A QUESTION OF PRIORITIES

A QUESTION OF PRIORITIES

PRIORITIES

New Strategies for Our Urbanized World

EDWARD HIGBEE

WITH AN INTRODUCTION BY
R. Buckminster Fuller

New York 1970

WILLIAM MORROW AND COMPANY, INC.

Copyright © 1970 by Edward Higbee

Printed in the United States of America.

Library of Congress Catalog Card Number 75–101701

Acknowledgments

The results of research are unpredictable. Preparatory work on this book began with a concern for the quality of America's physical environment. After a time it became apparent that pollution, blight, congestion, slums, and other visible forms of environmental ugliness are not isolated phenomena—therefore not susceptible to piecemeal solutions. They are the products of our culture—of our invisible values, motives, and beliefs as expressed in our institutions.

It is impossible to achieve the material abundance and spiritual freedom that could be attained in this Einsteinian Age while our minds remain convinced by Malthusian-Darwinian-Marxian thinking about scarcities. Our institutions are reflections of the ways we think and, in turn, our institutions shape our thinking. We are caught in a bind. Innovation is difficult because we are our own captors.

Because it took so long to work out the main ideas in this book I am most grateful to the Twentieth Century Fund for being patient. It was TCF which generously sponsored my research in its early stages. The result is not what we anticipated and our schedule was delayed.

I am indebted to Dr. John Osman and the Brookings Institution for opportunities to engage in urban policy seminars throughout the United States during the past six years. These meetings with America's business, political, and civic leadership have lent a sense of realism to what follows.

The influence of Dr. R. Buckminster Fuller's calculations for mankind's realizable success on what Bucky calls our "Spaceship Earth" will be evident to the reader. When I asked him if he would write the introduction it was to acknowledge this debt to his thinking and friendship.

As a special favor to me John Willey edited the manuscript, tightening up the original loose ends. Special thanks are due to the staff of the Library at the University of Rhode Island. Finally, I appreciate the careful secretarial work of Mrs. Margaret Anderson, Miss Stephanie Gillman, and Mrs. Leslie Samels.

To Holly and Heather

"The real question before Congress is one of priorities, of how we are to allocate our great but not unlimited resources among many important national programs."

—Senator William Fulbright as quoted in
The New York Times, October 16, 1963.

Contents

PREFACE		xiii
INTRODUCTION		xvii
Chapter 1.	The Technological Potential	1
Chapter 2.	Social Resistances	27
Chapter 3.	Toward a Theory of the City	55
Chapter 4.	Governments and Budgets	82
Chapter 5.	A Society of Responsibility	119
Chapter 6.	The Shell	160
Appendix	Sources of Quoted Material	199
Index		207

Preface

Species of human beings have been on earth for over a million years. For the first 99 per cent of that time survival depended upon adaptation of body and mind to the unmodified primeval landscape. Our early ancestors organized themselves socially into small, widely dispersed families, clans, and tribes so as not to overpopulate their natural environments. These primitives deliberately subordinated themselves to their own imagined gods whom they credited with control over every aspect of a mysterious natural world. Ancient taboos against tampering with things as they are, whether physical or metaphysical, remain powerful influences in our culture.

For the past 10,000 years, since the invention of agriculture, selected cultivated landscapes and more complex social organization have made it possible for larger populations to exist. The quantum jump in resource-making capability afforded by agrarian technologies led to a displacement of the institutions and the gods of pre-agricultural peoples. Any drastic change in the human environment brings into question traditional folkways, values, and beliefs. Being the psychic glues by which societies are stuck together, they must be relevant to the way things are or undergo transformation.

Now the world is in the midst of its second major ecological upheaval. The whole of humanity, with varying degrees of shock and success, is switching from an agrarian to an urban resource base—from a dependence upon the limited capacities of modified natural landscapes to a reliance upon inanimate energy technologies and complex, globalizing social institutions. Now it is apparent that survival depends upon how we relate to our enigmatic selves both locally and universally. We have become an interdependent world community, but our minds and institutions have not adjusted to this technological fact. Resources, as found in nature, will no longer support the mass populations now on earth. Even modern agriculture depends upon urbanization for its productivity.

Therefore, in this book, urbanization is regarded as an ecological process. It shapes our exterior environment but, more importantly, it reorganizes all previous systems of human association. It is revolutionizing the ways we think much to the distress as well as the benefit of individuals, communities, and nations. Again psychic glues have come unstuck and new ones are being invented that are more in accord with new realities.

In this context the city is regarded both as the product and the instrument of the urbanization process. Therefore the city is every urbanized community and its technology whether it be a metropolis, a suburb, or a space capsule orbiting the earth. While the physical shell of the city is inescapably visible, its invisible psychological make-up is infinitely more meaningful. It is our minds which create and manage our synthetic environment. The quality of that environment is a reflection of the synthesis we have made of ourselves.

Since new urban techniques of resource-production and institutional organization cannot be introduced into agrarian societies without threatening their total structure visibly and invisibly, the truest revolutionaries of our time are the managers of modern globalizing industries. In underdeveloped countries widespread social discontent results when cities begin to industrialize but do not evolve institutionally fast enough to incorporate into their organizational networks the populations which evacuate the countryside. Even in the United States our ghettos are jammed with farm refugees who are not yet viably affiliated with the institutions of our urban society.

For the city to become a universal ecological success, which it surely can be, present excessive spending on the military by governments of all nations must be curbed. The capital now wasted on warfare is required to build new resource-making urban technologies. The military approach to resource procurement and social organization is agrarian and obsolete. It favors the occupation of territories in order to extract their natural resources. It suppresses institutional change and enforces thought control. On the other hand urbanization, as it strives to be a successful ecological process, works toward freedom of thought and the global interdependence of all peoples.

As humanity becomes increasingly dependent upon its own man-made synthetic environment of integrated resource-supply systems it rejects the idea of military intervention. The superposition of force can gratify only those who remain committed to outworn political ideologies invented to cope with the resource scarcities of an agrarian age. Only the educated and ideologically uninhibited human mind is capable of inventing the technologies and institutions adequate to meet the needs of the world's new mass populations. It is to such invention via the research-development and design-science route that the public wealth of all nations should be applied.

In recent years the Pentagon alone has spent more tax money than all of America's 50 states and 70,726 units of local government collected to finance their public services. The Federal Government now collects two-thirds of the nation's total public wealth. Its current spending to cover the costs of past, present, and future wars amounts to four-fifths of its general administrative budget. A change of priorities is imperative.

An Introduction
by R. Buckminster Fuller

Though small of stature, Edward Higbee is invisibly mighty. He is a David who aims his sling unerringly to fell theretofore seemingly invulnerable, socioeconomic, bugaboo giants, irksomely blocking the broad highways along which evolutionary advances of ever larger numbers of humanity must be gained. But more about Higbee later. We must first identify the army of bugaboo giants he is now aiming to slay.

As we enter the eighth decade of the twentieth century, what the practical man means by reality is everything we can see, touch, hear, smell and taste. Throughout all history, up to a century ago, human beings have been held utterly responsible for their every waking deed. It was assumed that man was consciously controlling everything he did. Freud and Mesmer greatly shook this concept. They proved through hypnotism that men were often responding subconsciously to unfamiliar organic and psychological controls. The common criminal laws of man had to be changed to cope more logically with the subconscious, ergo, unblamable behaviors of man. Physics, chemistry, genetics, virology, physiology, neurology, ecology, geology and even astrophysics are combining to demonstrate that humans are myriad-frequency complexes of 99.9 per cent automated organic processes interacting with the universal environment. Dismaying as it may be to their ego-vanities, humans are less than one millionth of one per cent conscious of all that accounts for their successful growth, adaptation and survival. But that one millionth of one per cent conscious control can be, and sometimes is, amplified by the creatively inspired and unselfishly minded—to make importantly regenerative contributions toward humanity's subconscious success as well as to its conscious satisfaction, enlightenment and delight. As we shall see in due course, Edward Higbee is just such a contributor.

Though invented earlier, it was not until the beginning of World War One that human society began for the first time to employ radio and X-ray in everyday ways. In 1930 the first chart of the great electromagnetic spectrum was published. By then each and every one of the ninety-two regenerative chemical elements had been spectroscopically identified by their respectively unique incandescently disclosed electromagnetic wave frequency patterns. The great chart of the electromagnetic spectrum reality showed exactly where tin, iron, or copper is in the orderly scheme of Universe. This is where these hard metal realities really are identifiable in discrete mathematical interpositionings.

In this long chart, embracing also the gamut of long and short radio waves and all the different frequencies demonstrated by the different chemical elements, the arrangements are in the order of relative frequency magnitude. They range, as invisible "colors," from the very long, low-frequency waves towards ever shorter and higher frequencies. These frequencies, the subsensorial atomic weights and their unique and orderly electron, proton, neutron counts were, and will continue to be, the altogether invisible, but nonetheless most realistic, characteristics of all universal phenomena. Towards the high-frequency end of the chart there appeared a tiny little band of *visible* colors—red, orange, yellow, green, blue and violet. Then the visibility stopped again. These were the only frequencies which man had the innate equipment to tune in. Their lower-frequency neighbor in the spectrum community was infrared while their higher-frequency neighbor was ultraviolet. In respect to the total range of electromagnetic frequencies, we find that man's sensibilities tune in to less than one millionth of the total electromagnetic spectrum ranges of reality.

We can say that 99.9 per cent of everything that is going on today in research and science which is going to affect everybody's tomorrow is being conducted in the ranges of the electromagnetic spectrum which are completely invisible and are only instrumentally disclosed to man's senses. Consequently the common sense of "practically" reflexing humans as yet acknowledges reality to be only the one millionth fraction of actual reality. It is thus disclosed that common-sense-dominated humanity participates only subconsciously in the vastly ranging realities of universal evolution. Men used to be so motion limited in their total life's peregrinations that they saw an average of only one millionth of the Earth's surface. Living out their lives within the community limits, each human being knew approximately what all the other beings in the community were doing. They saw so much of one another that only the customs that could be tolerated by all tended to survive. Those who were physically strongest in the community were able to impose their will upon the others. The community learned to acquire tastes favoring that which was pleasing to the powerful masters and learned to accept that which was secretly displeasing to themselves. They also learned to forego that which the strong ones tabooed. There was nothing else they could do if they wanted to survive. Some independent souls sought to escape the local community and became known as shiftless vagabonds, no-goods, vagrants and gypsies. The master-accepted "good" man was the one who stayed at home and bought his own *real* estate-anchored home. Thus, tying individuals to the land rendered them highly exploitable while greatly adding to the liquid and remotely investible wealth advantage of the masters of the community. The masters of the community originally owned *all* of the land, having inherited it from those who originally claimed it by the power of arms. The more that the people exchanged their liquid wealth for the land and houses the greater was the new industrial tool-buying capability of the landlords. These statically isolated community conditions prevailed overwhelmingly when I was a young man. They held until World War One. In my 1913 freshman year's class of seven hundred at Harvard, only two of our class members owned automobiles. Their elders considered it improper for young people to have cars. Approximately all their families owned their homes with considerable lands about them. Automobiles were only for rich oldster bankers. In the whole world only a handful of rich young men owned automobiles.

Knowledge of the existence of great cities around our Earth was given to us through geography, but the great cities other than the one nearest to us were just magical names— something described to us glamorously in books or by the professional traveloguers.

Because science could not *see* what was going on in the copper wires of electrical generators and handled all invisible physics and chemistry exclusively by mathematical formulation, what science was doing was a form of highly accredited magic. To their intuitive dismay the Pandora's box of invisible science and technology had to be flung open by the power-structure masters of our planet at the time of World War One. They had to do so in order to save their world-around, ocean-surface network of lines of supply, which had been so effectively challenged by the outs' advanced use of science to innovate attack from underwater and from above the water. The energized world mobilization that caused it to be called "World War One" saw the beginning of the end of geographically isolated humans. It also saw the end of the rule of the world by sheer might. The great economic crash of 1929 occurred because those who had been running the world through mastery of the seas saw the airplane sink their armored cruiser. But to cap it all their operation of control only through the fraction of reality which could be mastered with their senses left them in utter ignorance of the significance of events transpiring in the invisible reality. They had to operate by relayed information received from liaison men who could not communicate adequately what it was that the scientist specialists were finding. The scientists, being specialists, could not see the integrated effects of their work. And the synergetic significance could not be ascertained by any of the old masters' command hierarchy. So they lost their world controls by default and never announced their loss of control. Since that time the great political states have vied for control but the static sovereign states are as obsolete as are the power masters who created them. World control can only be resumed by a new order of world man and he is now swiftly developing.

The world was integrated by radios, cables and transport systems of all kinds. Because World War One was centered in Europe it took a World War Two to make the Orient as well as all of the South Sea Islands a familiar place to any man, anywhere around the world.

The World War One unleashing of science and technology, which unexpectedly disclosed the vast ranges of the omni-interrelated, invisible reality of the electromagnetic spectrum's physical universe, also introduced to humanity structural and mechanical alloying and non-metallic chemical compounding of new substances in a major way. It also introduced mass-production technology. The alloys of metals and a myriad of new chemical compounds were progressively employed by man because each one demonstrated the capability of giving more performance for the same weight in ever lesser amounts of time while employing ever less energy per function. The swiftly increasing performance per units of invested resources changed things for all of humanity. And the chemical elements put into circulation did not get consumed.

They were used in one alloy association and then recovered and recirculated in new use form. Every time they get scrapped they are reused in such a way as to produce much greater performance. The process of recycling resources thus promises eventually to do so much with so little as to be able to provide all humanity with a better standard of living than any have as yet experienced or conceived. Some were benefited earlier and some later. Some have not as yet been benefited, but they soon will be if humanity does not go on making too many mistakes and is not too paralyzed by its earlier, fundamental-ignorance-conditioned fear reflexes—the ignorance being the personal lack of experience with which each of us is born. It is not derogatory to note that human life is born utterly helpless, and ignorant. This does not mean that the human child does not have superb equipment right from the start. But the child has to have a host of experiences from which to discover the extraordinary potentials, invisibly situate in the environment, which when discovered can be employed to make humanity progressively successful.

When I entered Harvard College before World War One my physics book had an appendix which had been glued in at the back subsequent to its machine binding. This appendix covered a new subject called "electricity." Electricity had been a part of academic physics for only five years. It must be remembered that the electron itself had not been discovered until the beginning of the twentieth century. After World War One electricity was renamed "electronics."

With the technology which continually produced more performance with less invested resources came industry's world-around recourse to chemical elements that men had never before employed. As we entered World War One the total number of chemical substances known to humanity was less than a quarter of a million. As we came into World War Two the number had multiplied to ten million. Since then the number has doubled. The human brain can only cope with something like ten thousand individually differentiated items within any fundamental category, for instance, the category of proper names of all the people they have met. Shakespeare used less than ten thousand different words in all his writing. No human brain can differentiate, store and retrieve such multitudes of data as that made available by the present myriads of scientific discoveries and contrivings by man within the computer-multiplied invisible realms of the electromagnetic spectrum reality.

To understand does not mean memorizing all the special case experiences. It does mean both apprehending and comprehending the family of generalized principles which permeate each and every special case experience to be considered. The computer can remember all the special case data and retrieve any of it in a flash, leaving the mind free to survey the data swiftly.

Overspecialized humanity fails to discern the significance and the discovery of generalized principles which have been discovered—in special fields other than their own. Overspecialized humanity, leaving its management to non-scientifically thinking and too shortsighted politicians, today fails to realize that its total organic success and its continued evolutionary development can only be regenerated by world man's access to the total inventory of chemical element sources wherever they may be. These sources are unevenly distributed by nature around the total face of our spherical spaceship Earth. The whole planet is involved in any of the great industrial complex developments. Just the common telephone transceiver instrument incorporates essential materials from four different continents of our planet. There is nothing in this omni-integrated involvement of the commonwealth of all humanity with all the resources which corresponds with the utterly obsolete concept of separate competitive sovereign states.

Until 1929, just before the great electromagnetic chart was published, in the year of the great economic crash, the number of American youths completing high school was still a very low percentage. Those going on into college constituted only a minor fraction of one per cent. The number of those going on to receive postgraduate master's and doctoral degrees was infinitesimal. Of all the extraordinarily accelerating curves characterizing social change nothing has been more impressive than the curve of the numbers now completing not only high school but college and going on to take master's and doctoral degrees. Man cannot conduct his affairs in the great invisible reality of the electromagnetic spectrum without the educated mind. Evolutionary demand for the capability to operate in the great invisible reality is such as to explain these great curves of educational acceleration. The master curve of educational acceleration is manifest everywhere around the Earth despite the ignorant discussions which I hear in America regarding the so-called underdeveloped countries. Americans seem to think of Africans only as naked with sticks through their noses. And it is the same for older people everywhere around the Earth regarding those in foreign parts. In contradistinction to such erroneous notions I find the student comprehension, and the quality of buildings and equipment of the universities in equatorial African countries, where I have gone as visiting professor—such as at the University of Science and Technology at Kumasi, Ghana, and at four universities in Nigeria and at others in the Congo, Uganda and Kenya—all to be equal if not superior in comparable aspects to American universities. I find their staffs of professors to be of the highest order—all Oxonians, Max Planck Institute, or equivalently educated Ph.D.'s. I have found the students everywhere around the world also to be of equally high capability regardless of the color of their skins. In my pre-World War One freshman class at Harvard University I think we had two foreign students. The number of foreign students was negligible, being less than a third of one per cent.

The percentage of foreign students now in all the colleges

and universities everywhere around the world is increasing very rapidly. Possibly this is the most swiftly increasing educational curve. Now many world universities have as much as 20 per cent of foreign students. This means that humanity everywhere is developing competent participation in the invisible-reality exploration and discovery. The young are developing everywhere as world citizens. The students are not talking about being world travelers. It is to them just normal to be a world traveler. It is normal for an ever increasing number of the students to have been enrolled progressively at universities on several continents of our planet.

During the summer when I was young we lived on our island in Penobscot Bay—ten miles from the mainland. The next human beings were two to fifteen miles away on other islands. Despite the distances there was a cohesive community. Each of those islanders knew the bay patterns of the lives of the humans on the other islands. For instance, we would see one another's boats go by on the weekly trip to the mainland for supplies, or we knew that this particular man went fishing in this particular area. So familiar with one another's patterns was each that, though they were scarcely ever near enough to see each other's faces, if one of those individuals failed to repeat his customary big bay patterning, then community concern was immediately felt and investigation was made by someone going to that island to see if the individual was all right. Others on other islands, seeing one going to check, kept their eyes trained for more clues to the situation. Thus the community operated in fundamental warmth of spirit even though individuals were quite physically remote. In fact, I would say that the friendship was warmer on the part of the individuals than it was in the tighter small-town urban community in which I wintered. In the bay there was much less careless criticism of the fundamental personal behavior patterns. You were rarely close enough to the other to make such small items of importance. Of course, you were sometimes visited or went to visit and could get a glimpse of the way the others handled their everyday problems. You tended to respect very much the other individuals' resourcefulness as each individual coped directly with nature. This same close kinship of those living remotely from one another was also manifest in the great western ranch life. Now, seventy-four years later in my life and on the other side of World Wars One, Two and invisible Three, which has just been finished, I find communities as yet intact but with different characteristics. This would be expected as we learn that reality has changed from sensoriality to invisibility. The communities are now more invisible than was that of pre-World War One Penobscot Bay.

My experiences in New York City, when I have to stay there from time to time and get in a subway, tell me how fantastically tightly human beings can be packed together. This experience makes it perfectly clear that proximity does not breed community. Thinking so is, however, a fundamental error of planners, politicos and do-gooders in general. You couldn't be more alone than you are in a New York subway train, jammed against people too closely to see their faces buried behind newspapers. It would be physically impossible for the human brain to cope with the number of cognitions and recognitions of all the personalities and the names of everyone he encounters in a great city. We meet millions in a few days and can only remember something under ten thousand in our whole lifetime. A modern community then is one in which the individual's friends are not the people next door. Even in the small university town where I have lived for the last thirteen years, Carbondale, Illinois, as a professor of Southern Illinois University, I find the university population, students and faculty, to be over thirty thousand. In addition, the town's population is twenty thousand. I do know where some of the professors and executives of the university live, but I don't know any of the people in the houses next door to us. We see each other from time to time, but we don't have time to even know each other's names because we are all just coming or going to our own lives' deployed patterns which are rarely on our own piece of land—that small little patch surrounding our house. The friends of individuals living in cities are not in the next apartments or in the next-door house or apartment house. Today our friends are scattered not only in remote parts of the city but are spotted all around the world. I travel around the world several times a year. I find that in every big town I have friends of yesteryear. It often happens that I have not met those friends in those countries in which I next find them. All of them are in such circulation that I find my community of friends is not only very large but also continually repositioning around our Earth. They dwell for a while here, then there, averaging at present about three years per location. Here at home the average American family is leaving town and going out of the state to another home every four years. That is the pattern of man. All today's attempts to identify community life statically in great cities in the terms of yesterday's pre-mobilization and pre-radio style of life are completely frustrated because the new dynamic world-community picture does not coincide with yesterday's close, isolated communities.

When the University of California students at Berkeley made front-page news by being the first students around the world to demonstrate great discontent with the educational system and the customs which dominate those institutions the newspapermen found the majority of them were in the junior class. I met with that particular group in 1966 in California and by mutual review of their case histories we found that its individuals were the first to be born with the television in operation. Television has been predominant in their lives. Each one listened to the people on the television for a thousand hours each year—which is many more hours than they listened to their own families and local friends. When their parents came home from work they told the children about the local store in which they worked and the troubles they were having in their business. The children found that they could go to the *third parent*, the television. "Who," on the hour, every hour, told them about the whole world's troubles and not about the little local frustrations. It told them about big frustrations of total man, and the compassion of all the young world for all of life was aroused by the problems of all humanity everywhere. It was clear to the children that the local problems were by-products of the bigger, world problems and could only be treated with effectively by total consideration and total recourse to total resources both physical and metaphysical.

The third parent, television, also told the children of the inventions which humans were developing around the earth and told them about the physical consequences of the invisible electromagnetic spectrum research and development. It told them about Van Allen belts enveloping our Earth's biosphere. The third parent, television, told the children, for instance, that man had now gone under the polar ice in an atomically powered submarine which could run for months and months with a very small amount of fuel. Soon after that it told the people that man had completely circumnavigated the Earth under the water in the atomic submarine without having to surface. Every day on the hour the television has been telling the children about all the extraordinary technical accomplishments of humanity. Children, intuitively integrating their awareness of all the problems of all of humanity around the Earth with their awareness also of all the technical capabilities which were manifest by virtue of the extraordinary expenditures made by the major nations of the Earth, but only under the auspices of preparations for carrying on war, said to themselves, "We feel that man could make his Earth work. We don't need war."

Not even knowing about Thomas Malthus, the children did not know that the fundamental raison d'être of all the great political states was predicated upon Thomas Malthus, the economist who in 1810 discovered that man was apparently multiplying himself much more rapidly than he seemingly could produce goods to support himself. Because bureaucracies do not think, but percolate through dogma, and because of this "officially" accepted but erroneous "fact," plus Darwin's "dictum" of "survival *only* of the fittest," all the great states as yet assume eventual trials at arms to discover which side is to have the opportunity to live a while longer. People throughout history have been dying far short of their potential life-span; that is, "average" man up to my father's time lived to no more than twenty-seven years, though he had a rarely attained potential of a hundred years. In view of this experience the great states have been saying that the "slow death" of slum rot and the fast death of war are equal and therefore wars are logical.

Under this fundamental assumption of ultimate Armageddon and mandated by mass-fear, the political leaders of all the powerful nations underwrite war-preparation expenditures that they could never authorize in peacetime. All the great technology which has been taken on by man in World Wars One, Two, and invisible Three has been acquired through man's saying he could only afford to do these things for defensive killing purposes. Humanity has not yet learned that it could afford to employ science and technology to make all of humanity a success. That has been universally assumed to be impossible—until just yesterday.

Until I was nine years old and the Wright Brothers had made their first flight, all the grown-ups told me and all the other kids that man would never be able to fly. It was inherently impossible—they explained. What is intuitively stirring all of young humanity around our Earth today is the realization that the assumption of impossibility of total success of man is a fallacy.

In the great new common-sense world of the young only the non-sense reality of the great electromagnetic spectrum is becoming logical. Because the young are thinking only about the invisible reality and the grown-ups only about the visible reality the latter cannot see what it is that moves their youth to abandon the old "tried and true" security dogma. The reality of the young is invisible to the reality of their elders.

What is stopping the young in the most profound and overwhelming way is the continued dominance of war affairs by the great sovereign political states, whose dogmatic bureaucracies are utterly committed to the Malthus-Darwin survival-only-of-the-fittest world warring. None of the sovereign states looks for what is good in one another and seeks to make all successful. So the altruistic youth are sucked into the fifty-billion-dollars-a-year pyscho-warring of the powers who seek to pervert the youths' idealism to their surreptitiously destructive ends. For the first time in history the great states have learned that because radar makes possible seeing the enemy send away his devastating rockets many minutes before the war heads hit, both sides can get off all their missiles before any of them arrive at destination, thus guaranteeing that both sides must lose. The present world warring is therefore entirely invisible. It is entirely psychological. It is to see who can most effectively destroy the other nations' credit around the world and how to disrupt the other one's economy and so arouse its youth against warfare that the other nation will drop its guard and fall. The U.S.A., NATO, Russia and China are altogether spending fifty of their combined one-hundred-fifty-billion-dollars-a-year war budgets in such psycho-warfaring. What has to go are all the sovereign political states. They are the bugaboo targets of Edward Higbee's sling shooting by his devastatingly cogent data. If the invisible "David" Higbee can shoot them down with his information stones, he will free humanity to live.

In the great invisible reality there are also a number of individuals whom we shall call "invisible men" who are doing the invisible but eminently important work for humanity. Every once in a while Nobel Prizes bring attention to the otherwise invisible individuals who are working in these areas. Thus is their work acknowledged. But for each one that is acknowledged there are millions who are doing equally important work that is not acknowledged. The establishment feels that it just cannot give thousands of annual Nobel Prizes in each and every category and still have the idea of a prize seem significant.

There are now multimillions of invisible men doing their invisible work in the great invisible reality. Most of them are specialists who as such do not comprehend the broad implications of their work. There *are* individuals who have greater understanding of the non-sense reality and of the great family of generalized omni-interaccommodative principles. They apprehend the trends and the checks and balances of nature which govern the rates of gestation of the birth of new evolutionary factors which for the moment seem to be frustrating the realization of the increasing success of humanity which nonetheless is trending swiftly toward the success of all. The men with clearer insights are usually those who have been less damaged at the time of their youth by the circumstances in which they developed.

One of the most important of the invisible men that I have been privileged to know seems to have had his faculties approximately undamaged by his youthful experiences. He is our friend Edward Higbee, at present Professor of Land Utilization in the University of Rhode Island's Department of Geography. Specializing in history and chemistry in his undergraduate college days, Higbee went on to do postgraduate work in geography, soil science and agronomy—studies integrating the experimentally gained knowledge of biology and chemistry and employing it toward the development of an ever improving food-energy support of humanity. After his U.S.A. graduation, he went to tropical America, where he spent several years studying and working on agricultural problems.

Back in the United States, Higbee's retrospective, long-distance reconsiderations of his previous experiences gave him an awareness of the significantly important pattern disparity between the East Coast U.S.A.'s independent farmer's economics and those of the great hacienda types of operation in Spanish-speaking and -customed America. He saw the vast contrast between the multi-thousand-acred lands of the hacienda whose prototypes were the feudal era's small kingdoms, baronies and overlordships. The owner of the land commanded its working by his peons. The hacienda's often even multi-square-miled land was to be contrasted with the New England and Eastern United States' farms of only twenty-five, fifty, or one hundred acres. In the Eastern United States, the sometimes owner—sometimes sharecropper—farmer worked his own land with only the help of his son, or possibly one or two paid hands. This was very different from the hacienda with its army of peons. Higbee saw that the pattern of the hacienda went all the way north from South and Central America into Mexico and then northward into California, where the lands once belonged to the Spaniards. He saw that the great fruit, cotton and other farms in California all followed the hacienda economics. In California the large numbers of men required to work the farms were drawn from the hacienda world of Mexico into California at crop time, giving rise to the great armies of foreign migrant workers. Higbee realized that the mammoth farm pattern of the West Coast was moving eastward of the Rocky Mountains and was taking a new dominant pattern in the wheat fields of the great plains states of Kansas, Nebraska, etc. Instead of the migrant workers, there was the migrating motorized industrial machinery on pneumatic wheels tended by relatively small crews of highly skilled radio-telephone-interconnected operators. For such operations farm ownerships of less than two hundred acres became uneconomical and were sold, vacated and consolidated into absentee ownership farms of thousands of acres. In this western and mid-central portion of the United States, the mechanized armies start out from Texas and Louisiana and move northward seasonally with their mass-production tools—first to do the planting. From their farthest north position the mechanical teams turn southward again with their harvesting equipment. The landowners need not be present at all. Great armies move overnight into the towns occupying all the motels and do the mechanized field working of the region in a day. Harvested crops go in trucks to central grain bins in the town, where weighing certificates are issued to the mechanical-harvester team master who goes to the local bank and collects his money. The harvests are handled by the banks on behalf of usually very distant owners. Thus, the farm houses of the western farms were abandoned.

Because the United States of America had been born on the eastern seaboard and had only gradually expanded westward, the original farm-owner pattern characterizing the vast majority of its early citizenry had brought about a political way of thinking which persuaded the politicians that the farmers always lived on their land and had the controlling vote of the nation. The voting districts' representation of Congress was evolved in those terms. Two decades ago Higbee saw that this legend of the superior power of the farm vote was still current, and because of it, the United States Congress continually made decisions intended to favor the farmer. He saw that the swift eastward sweep of the foreigner-worked or mechanized hacienda farming permitted absentee ownership, which meant in turn that there really was a negligible farm vote. Despite its fallacy, the Congress was as yet doing everything possible to help the only theoretically resident farmer, as, for instance, vast annual subsidies for non-planting to permit him high price stability. This greatly reduced the food production for a world in which more than half our planet's population is as yet undernourished or starving. This also meant that the small tobacco and peanut farmer in the South was not allowed to increase his twenty-five-acre planting. There was nothing he could do to increase his poverty scale earnings. It also meant that enormous sub-

sidies for non-planting were going to the absentee owners of
the vast acreages of the West. This meant that large fractions
of the money thus earned were being fed back into lobbies to
continue the legend that had become a deceit—that the farm
vote was of critical importance.

What is important about all of this recitation is that until
Edward Higbee came along, no one had been even mildly
effective in dispelling the now false legend of the political
power wielded by the farmers' votes. The farm subsidies go
on but only because of powerful tax and other lobbies.

Along with the explosion of the myth of the farm population comes the swift admission of the overwhelming urbanization of humanity.

Though threateningly noxious as are all the pollutions of
our physical environment, there is probably no pollution
quite so great as is the invisible, metaphysical pollution which
I call "the information pollution." Misconceptions over-
whelm the brains and frustrate the effective thinking of human society. Chaotically misinformed, society doesn't know
where to start with its physical pollutions. This is why democracy is in great trouble.

In this present book, Edward Higbee has tackled the false
concepts permeating urbanization. He has tackled it on a
sovereign nation basis. Using his great skills of comprehensive harvesting of fundamental data, he explodes myth after
myth employed in political maneuverings. His harvesting of
the world figures—as well as those of the United States—is
nothing short of breathtaking. No one has ever shown so
clearly that if the enormous expenditures going into war on
the part of all the major nations—in particular, U.S.A., Russia and China—were applied to livingry undertakings in as
boldly imaginatively a manner as that going only into kill-
ingry, all humanity could be a success overnight—and with
that success sustainable unto the nth generations of humans
to come aboard our Spaceship Earth.

A QUESTION OF PRIORITIES

1
The Technological Potential

Community

Tristan da Cunha, sometimes called "the loneliest island," lies far from the usual sea-lanes of commerce. It is a sparsely populated spot of sixteen square miles in the South Atlantic almost equally remote from Africa, Antarctica, and South America. There some 250 Tristanians, who are British subjects, pursue a self-sufficient way of life based upon an abundance of natural resources. Each family has its own house, land, cattle, sheep, and a fishing boat. Clothing is commonly homespun, since weaving and other subsistence handicrafts substitute for an industrial technology. A resident has described life on the island as "really a fine arrangement, giving a man balanced occupation—when weather was bad at sea we tended potatoes. When it was good we fished."

Until about two decades ago money was not used on Tristan da Cunha and taxes were unkown. In the century and a half since their ancestors first settled there Tristanians never built a jail or hired a policeman. They have said of themselves, "The worst thing we could do was to be unkind to anyone."

In 1961 this pleasant do-it-yourself existence was temporarily suspended. The eruption of a volcano forced all inhabitants to seek refuge in England. There in London they came face to face with the twentieth century. One refugee expressed bewilderment at having to cope with this new, more complex world: "It is like becoming children again. We shall have to start and learn from the beginning." Another marveled at the size of the telephone directory. To him it was inconceivable that there could be so many different names and such numbers of people in a single city. A third discouraged old gentleman complained, "I can tell you one thing that the people of Tristan have something to hold in life that you people can never hold, no matter how soon you try or how hard you try, and that is to live together as a community." He had grasped the fundamental problem of the modern city. In his simple terms of reference there was no solution.

Two years after their flight most Tristanians went back home. The volcano had subsided; some cattle and sheep had survived; fishing at sea was as good as ever. New "hutments" were built and life went on as before. Those who returned to their past were fortunate they had a past to return to.

This option is not available to most persons of a nine-teenth-century disposition who would like to escape from the magnitude and anonymity of modern urbanization to a simpler, more intimate community. A vastly multiplied humanity no longer fits into a tidy Tristanian ecological balance with nature. Population multiplication and the proliferation of cities where millions, instead of dozens, are sustained within a few square miles have altered forever the environmental prerequisites of the human race. Though the solution will not be easy the urbanizing world is trying to discover how to "live together as a community." It has no alternative. In the million years since mankind began to inhabit the earth it has known only three truly distinctive environments: nature's unmodified landscape, the farm, and the city. Each has required a special kind of knowledge, particular technologies, and unique systems of community organization. What is appropriate for Tristan da Cunha will not work for the city of London. London is irrelevant to Tristan. Yet in this the Tristanians are out of phase. How London works, and all the other metropolises of the world, must be the overriding concern of the majority of mankind. The city as a way of life is not a choice but a necessity. No other combination of technology and society will answer to the needs of contemporary mass populations.

The Synthetic Environment

Cities are ecological systems. They are environments that supply resources to their inhabitants. They afford food, shelter, and security, which every habitat must offer its inhabitants if it is to fulfill its biological role. The urban habitat is unique in that it is synthetic. Both its physical shell and its vital resource-making technologies are man-made. It is not a natural environment like the rain forest or a modified natural environment like the farm. To function effectively within this self-constructed environment the individual must be specially processed. He must be acculturated so that he fits. The more complicated and productive the synthetic habitat becomes through technological development the more complicated becomes the acculturation process. The man-made environment is suitable only for the properly man-made man.

To invent and organize the resource-making technologies of cities has demanded remarkable intelligence. But intelligence is what the human brain is supposed to possess. More demanding upon the brain than the resource-making technologies of cities is the invention of urban social institutions that enable mass populations to live together as communities. Since they did not exist during the hazardous millennia of biological evolution, we are not instinctively prepared for such aggregation. Man has a herd instinct which enables him to live in relative harmony with small numbers who are familiar—with members of families, clans, and tribes who behave predictably because they share a common culture. But this herd instinct has limits. It rejects the unfamiliar. As presently composed, high-density urban populations are usually assemblages of culturally distinct stranger-groups. They are critical masses of unfamiliar components and therefore potentially hostile to one another. It is the brain's job to invent appropriate social institutions that will interrelate the unfamiliar and thus allay instinctive fears and promote cooperation. Urbanization challenges mankind to invent a culture of compatibility for mass populations which, because of evolving resource-making technologies, must live at high densities in synthetic habitats.

Social institutions are survival mechanisms. Their biological function is to organize people and to so condition their minds that they may live within the constraints of their environments. But they are valid only as long as the constraints which generated them remain fixed. Let the constraints be changed through technological innovation, and they become irrelevant. Social organizations and all the folklore which sustains them must adapt to change or perish. Material technology and social organization are inseparable components of any environment. Therefore an age of technological revolution is bound to be an age of socio-cultural revolution. This book is concerned with the social consequences of technological change and their impact on the synthetic environment of the city.

Expansion

A hundred years ago there were twenty-six cities in the United States with more than 25,000 persons apiece. Of the national population of 40 million three-quarters were farmers and rural villagers. Today the total population is five times larger and nearly three-quarters live in metropolitan areas. Now there are 805 cities with populations of more than 25,000. Possibly in another hundred years there will be 3,000 to 4,000 cities as large as that or larger. Major cities today have populations of 5,000 to 15,000 per square mile. New York has 25,000 per square mile. Manhattan Borough has a density of 77,000 per square mile. Chicago has models in its planning office which demonstrate how concentrations of 90,000 could be physically accommodated—presumably in some post-Daleyian era when it has learned how to live together as a community.

Future urban densities need not follow the escalator. They might very well level off as the electron replaces the wheel, and physical aggregation may not be as essential then as it is now. The city of the future could be even more diffused than Los Angeles, which has an average density of 5,500 per square mile. Laserways for sending instant weightless messages might more efficiently replace freeways built for personal travel. Whatever the spatial pattern it will be inconsequential compared with the new techniques invented to interrelate human beings. Those techniques, not structural designs, will precondition the evolution of our culture and determine how we shall become a more coherent society. Guessing about the looks and physical layout of the city of the future is a peripheral amusement. Urban form will respond to human function—not the reverse.

Slums, pollution, congestion, and lawlessness are not the causes of urban decay. They are symptoms of deeper pathologies. The physical city is only a shell made to accommodate people and what people do. Change their way of life and the shell becomes disfunctional unless it, too, is changed accordingly. The sickness of cities is the result of their failure to change institutionally as fast as science and technology change the functions of people. Institutional obsolescence is at the root of physical obsolescence.

The Einsteinian Equation

The capacity of advanced urbanization for abundance and well-being is underwritten by the Einsteinian equation $E = MC^2$—energy is equal to mass times the square of the speed of light. When Einstein came to this conclusion in 1905 as the consequence of mathematical logic, even he doubted that mankind would ever discover practical ways to release, let alone harness, the fantastic quantities of energy locked up in the organization of matter. Many years later he remarked, "What I have done is of no practical significance whatsoever."[1] Yet $E = MC^2$ stated unequivocally that physical substance is pure energy compactly organized. The equation implied that if ways could be found to constructively manipulate this energy then all humanity could be freed forever from the fear of scarcity. With limitless inanimate energy under human control even the crudest and most abundant raw materials such as the earth's ordinary bedrocks and its sea waters could be made to yield inexhaustible quantities of usable elements. Even the elements themselves might be transmuted. The carbon dioxide in the atmosphere could be converted into sugars and its nitrogen could be transformed into proteins. The threat of hunger would be eliminated and any excuse for one human being exploiting another would be unacceptable in a rational society.

Studying Einstein's mathematics R. Buckminster Fuller as early as 1938 predicted that science eventually would discover how to release and constructively utilize nuclear energy. It would become, Fuller prophesied, "Mrs. Murphy's horsepower"; eventually physical drudgery would cease. Hiroshima came seven years later. A perversion of the Einsteinian equation by the world's great military powers had led to its application destructively rather than creatively. Nuclear diplomacy produced the cold war and continues to

[1] To R. Buckminster Fuller. (For sources of these quotations from Dr. Fuller and of all other quotations and supporting data not specified in the text, see notes, organized chapter by chapter, in the Appendix.)

threaten universal holocaust. The most rational statement ever made in the name of human welfare was and still is perverted to evil ends. While $E = MC^2$ says, "Science and technology can make all men free and amply supplied with essential goods" world societies, out of age-old habit, use it to intimidate one another as they once used spears to decide who should get the limited resources provided by nature. Our greatest intellectual enterprises and the largest share of our public treasures are expended to develop its destructive rather than its creative potential.

This is not the first time that the power of genius to do good has been turned to lethal ends by opportunists. Such perversions are products of the mind—they are psychological phenomena. They are not inherent in the objective data. It is the opportunity of the city to convert the potential for well-being of the Einsteinian equation into a reality. The primary obstacles are cultural; not technological. The success or failure of cities lies not in their misshapen shells but in their misshapen human contents. Our cities are a reflection of the ways we think.

If we persist in extolling the virtues, real or fictitious, of an outmoded agrarian past with its strictly limited resource capabilities while neglecting the potentialities of modern urbanization, which could create abundance, we will succeed in undermining the only kind of environment that might support mass populations adequately. It is not an exaggeration to suggest that the Einsteinian equation is the most significant single factor in the technological foundation of a successful urban ecology. It holds forth the promise that man can synthesize consciously what nature has stumbled upon fortuitously. It suggests that mankind can deliberately take charge of the evolution of its own environment and make it good. But urban plenty will not be brought into being by agrarian minds functioning in the context of obsolete agrarian institutions invented to ration scarcity. In the past, resources available to mankind were the products of land and physical labor. Wealth was measurable in terms of controlled populations and controlled territories. Now, through the evolution of science and technology, resources have become non-territorial. They are directly proportional to intelligence intelligently organized. Wealth has become the product of human talents educated to create rather than to exploit nature's limitations.

Acceleration—The Law of History

History provides a perspective with which to appraise the ecological significance of urbanization. Frederick Jackson Turner, foremost analyst of the role of the frontier in American development, acknowledged to a colleague toward the end of his career, "There seems likely to be an urban reinterpretation of our history." [2] The colleague, Arthur M. Schlesinger, Sr., credited the nineteenth-century American city with having nurtured "most of the humanitarian impulses of the pre-Civil War period. . . . From the cities came the effective energies behind the establishment of free public education, the more humane treatment of the insane, penal reform, the beginning of free public libraries, and the woman rights' movement. Such places also exerted an important influence on the struggle for manhood suffrage, the effort to abolish war, and the antislavery cause." [3] Above all, the city was a generator of economic enterprise which eventually would make worldwide abundance possible, if inconceivable to those of an agrarian outlook. By 1896 it was estimated that the average wealth of urban families in America was already three times that of rural families.

By 1920, only thirty years after the frontier had disappeared, the population of the United States was over one-half urban. By 1950 it was evident that machines were replacing manpower on farms so rapidly that within two decades it would become overwhelmingly urbanized. In 1904 historian Henry Adams identified "acceleration" as the law of history. Plotting the rising curve of man's control over inanimate energy, which is the technological heart of urbanization, Adams declared that "arithmetical ratios were useless for any attempt at accuracy." He employed the logarithmic scale. By allotting equal blocks of space to the last 100 years, to the preceding millennium, and before that to the preceding 10,000 and 100,000 years, Gerard Piel, editor of the *Scientific American*, has used Adams' exponential scale to show man discovering fire sometime in prehistory, perhaps 50,000 years ago, then harnessing waterpower about 5,000 years ago. Control of wind for mills came in the twelfth century A.D. Two centuries ago the industrial revolution began with the steam engine.

Not only had significant new controls over sources of energy followed one another at ever shorter intervals but each new means of control vastly multiplied the total inanimate energy put to work. After steam came the internal combustion engine. "Now," says Piel, "the first nuclear reactors are delivering electricity to the power networks of the world." The demand for electric power doubles every decade in the United States. By 1980 it is expected that nuclear reactors will produce 30 per cent of this country's output. On the logarithmic scale this succession of power systems yields a steeply rising curve of energy production that shows extreme acceleration in the last decade. "The exponential increase in the flow of mechanical energy through our economy," Piel observes, "has placed the equivalent of more than 100 human slaves at the disposal, on the average, of every man, woman and child. Less than half our labor force are employed as producers of goods; not much more than 40 per cent, if the production of armaments is subtracted from the total output. Factory workers will be as scarce as farmers in another generation. Our abundance is freed equally from the constraint of resources. The industrial order does not discover resources; it literally creates them." [4]

In the United States between 1950 and 1964 the production of electricity increased 176 per cent while the population grew 26 per cent. The retail cost per kilowatt advanced 10 per cent while general consumer prices advanced 29 per cent. The consumption of more cheap inanimate energy per man resulted in a substantial increase in real wages. In fact it helped the workman to earn more than his own efficiency warranted. While average wages advanced 89 per cent average efficiency increased only 49 per cent. Cheap energy not only makes work easier but, coupled to an improved technology, it adds almost as much to the standard of living as do workers themselves. The U. S. Bureau of the Census estimates that the population of the United States could reach 250 million by 1980. This would represent a 25 per cent gain over 1968. However, by 1980 each American will have twice the number of energy slaves that he had in 1968. Used constructively these slaves could within one decade abolish poverty, give every citizen complete insurance coverage to ease any misfortune, and create cities free of pollutions, convenient and safe to live in. Used to escalate the arms race their energies could be totally wasted.

To Henry Adams it was logical that knowledge accumulated at a rate which coincided with his calculations for the production of inanimate energy. This knowledge was not confined to science and technology but extended to an understanding of society as well. "No one could say that the social mind now failed to respond to new force," he wrote, "even when the new force annoyed it horribly." Looking backward into the nineteenth century and forward to the beginning of the twenty-first, Adams dreamed of a new kind of America. "At the rate of progress since 1800," he prophesied, "every American who lived into the year 2000 would know how to control unlimited power." Adams was familiar with Madame Marie Curie's discovery of radium and the enormous energy which radiated from it without an appreciable diminution of mass. Anticipating the Einsteinian equation Adams was confident that inanimate energy ultimately would be technologically limitless. Once he had such control over matter and energy Adams believed that the American of the twenty-first century ". . . would think in complexities unimaginable to an earlier mind. He would deal with problems altogether beyond the range of earlier society." [5]

It was clear to Adams what still is not clear to the majority of legislators and executives at the highest levels of political decision-making, namely that a new technology requires a new social context if its potential for well-being is to be translated into reality. Adams believed that this new social context would develop and prevail as inanimate energy became cheaper and limitless. If he had been right in that anticipation as he was in his anticipation of technological progress there would not now be in America such a wide discrepancy between the resource potential of an urban environment and its low level of achievement. We have come into an advanced urban age while our social attitudes and institutions remain agrarian.

Agrarian institutions are too few in variety, too simple in structure, and too personal in management to serve properly the diversity, complexity, and anonymity of life in urban America. A new technology, if it is to translate its resource potential into reality, requires a new society structured to implement that potential. The city, like any other ecological system, is the interaction between habitat and inhabitant. For any man to be viable in the city he must be able to coordinate his personal behavior with the behavior of the whole. He must fit. His actions must relate to the interactions of the total ecological complex. He must become an organization man to survive. This can neither be automatic nor easy because the institutional network of the synthetic environment is made unstable by technological evolution.

Arnold Toynbee defines society as a system of relationships between human beings who are not only individuals but also social animals who could not exist at all if they were not members of a group. "A society," he explains, "is a product of the relations between individuals, and these relations of theirs arise from the coincidence of their individual fields of action. This coincidence combines the individual fields into a common ground, and this common ground is what we call a society." [6]

Urbanization as a social process accommodates ever more numerous individual fields of action and by so doing develops a more heterogeneous "common ground." Thus urbanization is more open-ended than any antecedent system of human organization and, by being open-ended, has a better chance to become even more adequate as an environment rather than less so as populations increase, diversify, and specialize. In fact this open-endedness or capacity for mutation has already led to such a multiplicity of opportunities and interests that it is no longer possible to trace with precision the endless institutional relationships that keep coming into being and linking themselves to the network. But the urban ecological system is also vulnerable, particularly to the ideologies of scarcity held over from our agrarian past. These ideologies endorse aggressive individualism rather than cooperation—competition and rivalry rather than joint venture—dissension rather than agreement. Arthur M. Schlesinger, Sr., viewed the urbanization of colonial America as the prime generator of the social unity which made a new Republic possible. "The necessary concern with the general welfare contravened the doctrine of individualism and nourished a sense of social responsibility. This training in collective action, constantly reenforced by the everyday contact of the citizens in less formal undertakings, assumed a commanding importance as the Revolution approached." [7] The development of a "sense of social responsibility" is still the city's most vital service function. The material resource potential of the Einsteinian equation cannot be achieved except through the institutions of a society of responsibility.

If, for lack of faith in abundance through technological progress or for lack of faith in the capacity of society to be responsible, urbanization should fail to accommodate all the world's expanding populations within its ecological system as it evolves, it could strangle humanity in an authoritarian tyranny more rigid than anything it has heretofore experienced. The increasing concentration of specialized brain power in ever more complex organizational networks—many now extending around the world—leads to the coordination of international resource-making systems. This globalization of resource manufacture opens up the prospect that all underdeveloped nations may indeed become developed by urbanization. It also suggests that the age of contending militaristic blocs is ending. For a long time humanity has regarded war as ethically wrong. Now it becomes increasingly clear that it is an obsolete political stratagem. Once the entire world becomes dependent upon its cities both as sources of resources and as the organizers of populations it will not be possible to destroy them without committing suicide. By creating a universally interrelated and interdependent synthetic environment to sustain it mankind commits itself to be rational regardless of how irrationally it has behaved in the past. The military mind, already frustrated by this prospect, is actively researching biological warfare techniques that would eliminate people without destroying their urban shells. What that simplistic, single-track mind does not apparently comprehend is that the urban shell and its resource-making techniques are functional only within a coexistent social context. Destroy that human organizational network of relationships and the material shell would be useless, its technology unworkable.

Globalization

To make the best use of manpower, capital, and technology the world now is witness to a massive exportation of routine, labor-intensive jobs from developed to underdeveloped countries where wages are cheaper. The United States, the

USSR, and other advanced industrial states have established technical schools abroad with their own funds to train peons and peasants to perform industrial jobs that used to be done at home. At the same time all technically progressive countries are importing high-priced brains from wherever they can be lured, chiefly by pirating one another. International airways have become brain shuttles.

These worldwide redistributions of tasks, investments, and talents are the rational consequences of technological sophistication. They are dictated by opportunities for economic efficiency which always exist in any environment undergoing improvements in the techniques of material production and human organization. By globalization the maximum efficiencies of scale can be achieved. Increased scale underwrites mass production systems which in turn can be streamlined by specialization. Using the globe's cheapest labor and best brains in integrated mass production systems tends to maximize outputs through highest efficiency at lowest cost.

For example, keypunching is the human bottleneck in computer systems. No one has invented a way to skip the manual operation of transferring raw data to punch cards or tapes so that computers can read. This human input adds greatly to the cost of computerized operations. The wages of keypunchers in the United States run about $500 a month. However, the Computer Input Corporation has developed a cut-rate solution. It has trained girls in Bangkok, Thailand, to keypunch American business data for $50 a month. Computer Input flies raw data from any American city, gets the cards punched in Bangkok, then flies them home across the Pacific to its clients—all within five days. It is very simple. The girls do not understand English—neither does the computer.

Businessman J. Karl Meyer heads Development Authority for Tucson's Expansion—DATE. His organization is a "nonprofit corporation representing a broad cross section of the Tucson community." DATE plugs what is called the "Twin

Plant concept." The program induces industries from interior industrial cities to set up shop in Tucson, which is near the Mexican border. "You don't have to go to Hong Kong, Taiwan, South Korea or Japan for low-cost easily trainable foreign labor," says DATE. "It's available right here . . . along the Mexico-Arizona border for as low as 30 cents an hour in virtually inexhaustible numbers." Under the "Twin Plant" system components are manufactured at a Tucson location, assembled in nearby Nogales, Mexico, and then returned to Tucson for final inspection, packaging, and shipping. "Duty," says DATE, "is imposed only on the added value of the assembly." [8]

Among the first border cities to develop the twin-plant system was Laredo, Texas, which reports on the success of Transitron Electronics Corporation, which was persuaded to leave its former home in Wakefield, Massachusetts. Transitron now has a plant in Nuevo Laredo, Mexico, just across an international bridge from Laredo, Texas. The company uses a small specialized U. S. work force trained in the "electronics field" to manufacture products in its factory on the American side and a routine labor force of 1,400 Mexican nationals in its twin plant across the Rio Grande. The company specializes in communications equipment for the Defense Department.

Similar operations, differing only in product and local color, but not in organizational technique, are sponsored by all developed nations in a multitude of underdeveloped countries: in Spain, Brazil, Syria, Egypt, Korea, Greece, Ireland, Cuba, and Guatemala. Throughout the West Indies SEA TRAIN and SEA LAND trailer trucks, ferried by the hundreds aboard specially designed shuttle ships, deliver raw materials from the United States to the very doors of factories on the islands; then they reload with finished products at the same factories and return immediately to the mainland. A complete round trip from the Port of New York to a tropical factory takes slightly less than one week.

In Thailand the profit lure reaches 25 per cent or more. Among companies building and planning there are General Electric, Eastman Kodak, Gulf Oil, Chrysler, John Deere, Union Carbide and others. The Soviets are doing the same thing from India to Cuba. After Premier Aleksei N. Kosygin visited India in 1968 new orders for Indian exports from plants built with Soviet capital were, in the words of an Indian official, "stupendous." One order called for 600,000 tons of steel from a Russian-built plant; another, for 40,000 railroad cars. "It's a new kind of aid," remarked a trade analyst. "You build a plant, then you guarantee that you will keep it working to capacity." The financing country gets its routine work done abroad for less than it would cost at home. The underdeveloped country gets jobs.

G. Lawton Johnson is vice president of Boyden Associates of New York City, an international consulting firm and executive search service. "Intelligent expansion of industry by talented managers is the solution to most of the world's problems," Johnson says. "One of the most significant changes is the mushrooming globalization of industry, the worldwide spread of America's giant corporations. . . . The biggest mistake an American businessman could make today would be an unwillingness to probe, to understand, and to prepare his company for the vast challenge of international commerce." [9]

Underdeveloped countries everywhere appeal for foreign investment, offering as inducements low taxes and cheap labor. The Barbados Development Board urges industrialists in technically advanced countries to set up branch plants on the island, where "You can take advantage of an educated, easy-to-train labor force—surprisingly high productivity at surprisingly reasonable wage rates. . . . Pay no income or trade tax for ten years. And when you finally start paying taxes, it's a not-hard-to-take $12\frac{1}{2}\%$."

In March, 1969, Mr. J. A. H. Saunders, Chairman and Chief Manager of the Hong Kong and Shanghai Banking Corporation, reported to his stockholders. Exports from

Hong Kong, which had been increasing at an average rate of 15 per cent annually for some years, jumped to 25.8 per cent in 1968. "The growth of exports of clothing and also of electrical goods, though in both cases over 30 per cent, was outpaced," said Chairman Saunders, "by that of shipments of toys and wigs and of innumerable lesser items such as watches, locks, pleasure craft, cameras and binoculars. The wide variety of goods produced is a source of strength since any successful single line is liable to meet pressure for a restraint agreement."

Speaking of the industrial potential of underdeveloped countries in general Saunders observed, "The sensible course for these countries would seem to be to develop first industries which can capitalize on the one resource which they have in abundance and the advanced countries have not—a large, willing and relatively inexpensive labour force. Such industries should be able to be fully competitive on world markets."

Among its diversified interests the conglomerate Litton Industries operates a worldwide business machines and equipment manufacturing network. In addition to its American plants Litton is established in Britain, Spain, Belgium, West Germany, the Netherlands, Italy, Sweden, Canada, and Mexico. This business machines organization consists of 114 factories, yet it is only one division of Litton. In charge is Mr. Ralph O'Brien, senior vice president of the parent concern, who sees the need to place factories where conditions are right for the particular jobs to be done. The world can be a unified multinational production-distribution system and is becoming one. "The thing is to recognize the economic environment you're in rather than to fight it," says O'Brien. As a result some Royal typewriters which entail high labor costs are made in Britain, Japan, and the Netherlands for the American market. Computer systems, in which design and engineering inputs are high, are made in the United States for worldwide sale.

Brain Drain

Natural resources have until recently been the mainstay of mankind. Humanity got along with what nature provided. Natural resources are tied to geographic place and they are unevenly distributed around the world. To control nature's raw materials the places must be controlled where they are found. That was the logic of nineteenth-century imperialism. Great nations assembled colonies which supplied them with natural resources mined, gathered, or grown by cheap peon labor. Now science and technology demonstrate that the term *natural resource* is relative. The more sophisticated the manufacturing process becomes the more natural resource suppliers become dependent upon it instead of the other way around. The organizers and managers of the world's manufacturing networks can assure themselves of raw material supplies more economically by investing in their development wherever the "economic environment" is right rather than by stationing a military occupation force to create a political colony. This fact persuaded France to withdraw from Algeria, Britain from India, Russia from Mongolia, and the United States from the Philippines.

The more advanced a nation's technology becomes the less it is dependent upon resources that are directly usable in their natural state and the more it relies upon invented systems of converting cruder, cheaper, more abundant raw materials into usable resources. The more advanced a nation's technology becomes, the less dependent it is upon human drudgery and the more dependent it is upon scientific and technological intelligence. A nation which attracts brains attracts the capacity to create resources through refined technological processes. Its potential for well-being is measured not by the numbers of people it controls or the extent of its geographic spaces, but rather by its success at collecting brains and using them. If there is a twentieth-century equivalent of imperialism it is brain-collecting.

Using a costly military establishment pre-World War II Japan was able to occupy Manchuria and Korea, yet even that extended geographic base could not satisfy her appetite for natural resources. A further pursuit of the military-occupation, cheap natural-resource approach led to Japan's assault on Pearl Harbor, and eventually to the defeat of her empire. Since then she has spent less than 1 per cent of her gross national product on the military. Instead she has invested heavily in the development of mines, forests, fisheries, and oil fields around the world which previously were unexploited for lack of capital, intelligence, markets, and qualified management.

Today Japan is a major producer of lumber and minerals in Canada, petroleum in the Middle East, fish in Peru, and iron ore in Australia. "Japanese Business Winning Where War Lost" blared a recent front page headline in Australia's authoritative *The Financial Review*. Now the Soviet Union has invited the Japanese to join in the development of Siberian industry. The switch from investment in military force to investments in economic development through applied intelligence does not reflect a change in ethics so much as a recognition of the changed nature of advanced industrial technology and the globalization of economic networks.

The international flow of scientific and professional manpower—the brain drain—is the most significant of mankind's recent migrations. Obviously its importance lies not in numbers, which are small relative to world populations, but in the strategic role which intelligence plays in an urbanizing world. In 1967 some 42,000 professional persons migrated to the United States from all over the world. Between 1962 and 1967, Taiwan alone lost 14,300 engineers, technicians, and other skilled minds—"the very ones," complains the *China News*, "whose service is most urgently needed" at home. Of these Taiwanese emigrés about 2,000 annually have been new university graduates who ranked in the top 15 to 20 per cent of their classes.[10] Jean-Jacques Servan-Schreiber, editor of the French magazine *L'Express,* says that in creating the wealth of industrialized states, "The one really important natural resource is gray matter." [11]

Brains are at a premium and will continue to be because supplies of high-grade, directly usable natural resources decline while consumption rises. The only possible way to keep mankind from running out of necessities is to invent and install new technologies which can produce more useful commodities out of low-grade, plentiful, but otherwise unusable raw materials. Synthetics make it possible to shift dependency from a scarce article to something plentiful. Getting more copper from ores of lower copper content is a matter of intelligence. The first mines exploited in Michigan's Keweenaw Peninsula in the mid-nineteenth century are said to have contained up to 60 per cent copper. The most recent mines opened in Arizona profitably produce copper from ores with three-tenths of 1 per cent metal. To develop new techniques and to organize them into production systems is a big part of what the synthetic environment of the city is all about.

Rebellion and Development

In 1966 World Bank president Robert S. McNamara, then U. S. Secretary of Defense, addressed an international audience in Montreal. He observed that during the previous eight years there had been 164 armed uprisings by indigenous people against 82 governments in underdeveloped countries. By contrast, only one such revolt had taken place against the government of an urban-industrial state. Per capita incomes in underdeveloped countries, said McNamara, averaged $170 per year. Rich nations he classified as having a minimum per capita average annual income of $750. The United States then averaged $3,500 per year per capita and was gaining at the rate of approximately $250 per year per capita. Clearly populations averaging $170 per capita annually can have little in common with populations earning $750, let alone with Americans whose ability to make more with less *increases* by at least $250 per capita annually. Revolts in underdeveloped countries and riots in the ghettos of U. S. cities have a common denominator. As the whole globe shifts from its outworn, inadequate agrarian way of life to the more productive urban environment great masses of people are left stranded. They are not needed on the soil, yet they can find no functional place in the city. Since they will not accept deprivation in the midst of growing affluence they resort to violence.

A sensible solution to this problem would be to accelerate the pace of urbanization and to prepare mass populations for effective roles within the institutional networks of cities. Suppression by the military and police may work for a limited time, but if in that interim superfluous people are not processed into functional members of the world community the inevitable eruptions will be cataclysmic. Possibly Robert McNamara's own request to shift his personal efforts from military suppression to economic development via the World Bank reflected a deeper understanding. After assuming his new post McNamara was asked if the Western world has the resources with which to develop the economies of underdeveloped countries. "There is absolutely no question about it in my mind," he replied. "One has to bear in mind that it may not be resources alone that stand in the way of achieving a satisfactory rate of economic advance in the developing world. It may well be that adaptation of political institutions, social reforms, and other actions within the developing nations themselves form a limiting factor." [12]

In India peasant bondage or debt peonage is known by several names: Banihari, Goti, Kamyoti, and Bannai. The name differs with region but not the system. Once a tenant becomes indebted to his landlord he must repay him with interest before he seeks to work for anyone else. Since the landlord sets wage and interest rates, peasants become tied to their lords' estates. If a man dies without paying his debt, his son inherits it. Known by other names this same system of human bondage may be observed throughout the under-developed agrarian world, including Latin America. While nominally illegal in most countries, the laws forbidding peon-age are not enforced on the feudal estates where traditionally the landlord or his designate is the local judge. The best means of escape for those who want freedom is to sneak off to the cities.

Whatever the power of the armed forces arrayed against them, it is hardly likely that the 2.4 billion restless poor of the underdeveloped world will remain indefinitely intimi-dated. Rather than push their frustrations to the limit, it would be better to accelerate worldwide urbanization and the dissolution of the caste-bound institutions of agrarian states. However, it will be as difficult to dissolve the impedi-ments to rational social change as it is to deal with outright rebellion. The élites whose privileges are rooted in the es-tablished hierarchical structure of their societies are not about to challenge the *status quo* which favors them. Military commanders are, of course, members of the élite.

Writing in the *Washington Sunday Star,* Jeremiah O'Leary quotes an unnamed but knowledgeable public official who sees this fact as the reason for the failure of the U. S.-Latin American Alliance for Progress. "The Alliance and the United States," he explained, "are committed to both revo-lutionary change and to the stability of the *status quo* and this is a paradox we can no longer live with." It is this funda-mental contradiction of ends which has precipitated the mili-tary coups that seek to forcibly reconcile the irreconcilable. This same contradiction has prevented a resolution of the Vietnam war. Behind its military shield the United States has professed to seek a change in the *status quo* that would offer the common people hope, but the generals Thieu and Ky are as opposed to peaceful evolution as they are to outright re-bellion. Of course, popular support of rebellion would vanish if the agrarian feudal system were to dissolve by peaceful change. But rather than alienate the generals and the landlords, American officialdom has alienated the people—it has consented to Communist-style, government-picked political parties and candidates who, when duly elected, are of no mind to reform outmoded feudal institutions.

Industrial urbanization by introducing hope precipitates crises in underdeveloped nations. The rural landless, seeking a better life, flock to cities before there are enough jobs for them and before they are trained for jobs. Pileups of surplus people in slums provoke cries that urbanization is a curse. The real curse is that cities, with their more adequate resource-supply systems, do not develop fast enough to absorb, train, and employ the hordes trying to escape from agricultural slavery. In the city they assemble into visible, frustrated, volatile masses which learn to articulate their misery and protest. In the country they are dispersed, hidden, and silenced. Since technological revolution provokes social revolution, the truest radicals of our times are urban industrialists and their globalizing economic networks which upset the *status quo* by offering the rural poor the hope of better paying jobs than the landholding élites of feudal societies have provided.

In a biological sense the city represents the highest form of ecological development. Through its ever-improving science and technology it multiplies resources beyond any previous possibility. At the same time, because it makes it possible for more people to live at higher densities, urbanization forces social innovation. It forces mass populations to discover new ways to live together as a community—ways which neither hunting-gathering nor agrarian societies required. The simple face-to-face relationships which work on Tristan da Cunha are impossible to achieve by the anonymous millions of a modern metropolis. What was personal on the farm must become impersonally institutionalized in the city. The more the techniques of urbanization supersede the techniques of earlier agrarian societies the more interdependent become the institutions of all men everywhere. It is already apparent that newly evolving international networks of institutions are becoming more significant in the production of resources and the organization of mankind than the local, geographically limited institutions of a vanishing agrarian age. The multinational corporation has superseded family enterprise.

Upgrading

If the reallocations of brains and cheap wage jobs now going on around the world were coordinated with social change and accelerated, then standards of living everywhere would rise. In backward countries, the chance to do low-skill factory work is a bonanza to peasants and peons who otherwise have no alternative but to do manual farm chores for landlords at slave wages. Any factory worker tending a power-driven machine is more productive and better off than a peon wielding a machete with his own muscles. Thirty cents an hour is better than thirty cents a day. An accelerated globalization of industry is the brightest hope of the underdeveloped world.

Within technologically advanced countries, which everywhere now export low-skill tasks with the intent of putting the finished products on the world market, the obvious need is to give their own citizens something better to do requiring greater skills and paying better wages. A report which Senator Edmund S. Muskie brought to the attention of the Congress estimates that sales by American corporations operating through subsidiaries in foreign lands may now amount to five times the value of all U. S. exports from our own shores—possibly as much as $165 billion annually. Sales of manufactured goods alone approximate $50 billion.[13]

No hillbilly white in Appalachia, Indian in New Mexico, or Negro in Harlem can stay alive on a wage that supports life in Hong Kong or Bangkok. Therefore, when 1,000 jobs move abroad that might have been done in America, they would have to be replaced by 1,000 better jobs at home. And 1,000 people would have to be better educated so that they could perform the new tasks. If the urbanization process fully realized its technological potential, this would happen. It would be good for everybody everywhere to be upgraded another step. It is the only way that underdeveloped countries will emerge from their feudal-agrarian dead end. It is the only escape hatch for Americans caught in urban ghettos and rural slums.

Any expectation that unemployment or underemployment in the ghettos of Newark, Chicago, or Oakland will terminate upon a faster rise in America's gross national product is idle dreaming in the face of the international exchanges of jobs, brains, and resources now taking place. Domestic policy in all nations has become inseparable from foreign policy. The international roles of underdeveloped and developed countries are being dovetailed as the world's economic resources of manpower, capital, and materials are organized into more efficient global systems. It is technologically rational for the world's labor-intensive, low-skill jobs to be done in low-wage countries where labor is in greatest surplus and capital must be imported. It is technologically rational for research, planning, and management skills to be concentrated in urbanized countries where the infrastructures of intelligence-generating services are sophisticated. But what is technologically rational must be matched by what is socially rational or the result could be a worldwide ecological catastrophe. A failure to realize that foreign policy is domestic policy and vice versa could be suicidal.

The immediate attentions of nations appear to be focused upon the short-term profit advantages to be derived from international technological rationalization. Discounted are the widespread social dislocations that new technological efficiencies precipitate in all countries whether they be developed or underdeveloped. The immediate reactions of dislocated peoples are to riot and rebel. The first reflex of those who feel their privileges threatened by change is to call out the military and the police. While economic rationalism offers the greatest prospect of resource abundance, a corresponding social rationalism is essential to put the resources within the reach of all. The social fabric of every country, rich or poor, is destined for major change. Vestigial agrarian institutions must go through their death agonies and new urban institutions must be born out of experimentation.

2
Social Resistances

Psychology

After a long countdown at Cape Kennedy on March 22, 1965, the jets of the sleek Gemini 3 spacecraft released their fury. The glistening shaft began its liftoff for a trajectory into the cosmos. There it released a 7,000-pound capsule manned by the astronauts Major Virgil L. Grissom and Lieutenant Commander John W. Young. The astronauts and their capsule then circled the earth three times before braking rockets tumbled them safely out of orbit and into the Atlantic Ocean only a few miles from a predetermined rendezvous. The flight was the culmination of two years of preparation which had employed the top talents of more than five thousand American corporations. The capsule alone involved the cooperation of 3,196 subcontracting companies, which supplied $348,887,-143.88 worth of parts and services. The project was a triumph of technology and organization. The whole nation followed its flight by radio and television. It took less than five hours from launching pad to splashdown. The distance covered exceeded 75,000 miles.

On the same March 22 a little band of three hundred freedom walkers took all day to hike sixteen miles along a narrow stretch of Highway 80 in the Black Belt of Alabama. These people were in the midst of a 54-mile journey from Selma to Montgomery that would take them four days. Their purpose was to present a petition to Governor George C. Wallace asking that he exercise his executive authority to secure to Negro citizens of his state the civil rights which legally had been theirs for over a hundred years but which were commonly ignored by the law's enforcers. On the same night that the nation honored its astronauts, the freedom walkers slept uneasily in a field in Lowndes County guarded from jeering segregationists by a ring of U. S. Army and National Guard troops. According to the Reverend Andrew Young of the Southern Christian Leadership Conference, white terrorism in the Black Belt had been so unrestrained that until late in 1964 "not a single Negro in Lowndes County had even tried to register [to vote] in the last 65 years." After the march to Montgomery, as freedom walkers were being ferried back to Selma by automobile, Mrs. Viola Liuzzo of Detroit, Michigan, was murdered on Highway 80 because she had participated in the march. Her assassin was never convicted although an F.B.I. informer told the court and jury that he was in the murderer's car at the time of the crime and saw him shoot. The black people's petition obviously had not altered the attitudes of those locally responsible for upholding law and order.

The flight of Gemini 3 and the spirit of Lowndes County symbolize the gap between America's technical capacities and its social resistances. While scientific knowledge accelerates at the logarithmic rate noted by Henry Adams and Gerard Piel, the equitable distribution of its benefits throughout society plods along by arithmetic progression. The divergence of these two rates of change tends to divide the nation even more severely at a time when it is in greatest need of comprehensive organization. To build a physical metropolis with functional unity for a split society is no easy task. A society divided into cultural isolates cannot agree on how to arrange its common habitat. What is illogical, disfunctional, polluted, and ugly about the contemporary city cannot be attributed to technological deficiencies or lack of resources. Rather it is the failure of society to organize itself so that the opportunities of material technology can be utilized.

In the spring of 1968, a distinguished group of systems analysts-engineers met in Washington. They and their colleagues are responsible for assembling diverse talents and putting together the complex organizations that build the nation's space hardware. Those at the meeting had been selected at preliminary regional forums sponsored by the 32,000-man American Institute of Aeronautics and Astronautics and the 7,000-man Operations Research Society of America. They came at the invitation of Vice President Humphrey, who urged them "to become more involved in solving our problems here on earth . . . to make our society a better place to live."

After three days of high-powered seminars on "Systems Analysis and Social Change," the results were summarized by Joseph H. Engel. "As we move closer and closer to human beings, human life, and to its goals," said Engel, "we find that we are dealing progressively with more and more difficult problems." The men who had mastered interplanetary space thought it would be more difficult to get off the ground with earthly problems. "We're very good at hardware and tactical problems and starting well-defined research and development programs. We're lousy at strategic and philosophical problems."

After exploring such "living" problems as riot control and slum removal, Engel said the conference concluded that "We need to put all of our psychologists, all our 'people-oriented' people to work on these problems. I see a very long and difficult road ahead." [1] The conferees had noted that a "system" is a harmonious arrangement or pattern. A modern social complex such as a city, however, has little of the arrangement and none of the harmony of that definition.

The Rand Corporation is one of the country's oldest, most

prestigious "think tanks." When it runs into tough problems, the Department of Defense calls on Rand to produce answers. In 1968, Rand agreed to think about New York City for two years for $2.4 million. While embarked upon the second year of its contract, the company came to the conclusion that national defense systems are simple by comparison with urban analysis. "This has certainly been an education for the Rand Corporation," remarked Douglas Scott, information director of the New York City office. "There were certain comfortable simplicities about research on defense but not here. The complexity of the human element, the complexity of the fiscal and political element, the plain complexity of New York City, are something we haven't encountered before." For its continuing analysis of New York, Rand uses a forty-man staff based in the city. Also it retains an additional forty scientists, engineers, and economists, some of whom operate at the company's headquarters in Santa Monica, California, while others are at universities throughout the United States. The one question Rand is not willing to analyze is whether or not its research will solve the city's problems. "The answer to that has to come from the Mayor," says Mr. Scott.[2]

Robert W. Glasgow, senior editor for Communications/ Research/Machines, Inc., publishers of *Psychology Today,* observes, "There is a profound psychological dimension to the acute problems of urban society. The 'alienation' of the various social units within the metropolis, the 'withdrawal' to the suburbs and the 'pathology' of racism—the very use of these terms is as precise psychologically as it is metaphoric." [3] Francis H. Horn, president of the Commission on Independent Colleges and Universities, State of New York, believes that the attitude of people, including an innate inclination toward irrationality, is the chief problem of the city. In Dr. Horn's view, a major social function of education is to train the mind to counterbalance a primitive irrationality with objective reasoning. A good educational background in the humanities is desirable for everyone, not just to enrich the individual life but as social insurance against mass misunderstanding. Without such a background the crowding process of urbanization which forces persons of diverse cultural programming together leads to mounting friction. The more interfaces, the more intense the reaction and the greater the need for a common denominator of culture to interrelate the differentiated.[4]

Such complexities conventional city planners are not trained to cope with, and this accounts for the fact that their usual solutions, conceived in terms of physical designs and structures, do little but prescribe cosmetics where genuine social psychoanalysis is required. Sociologist Scott Greer believes that "scared, or hostile whites . . . are the major social problem of American society."[5] They are the majority, and the policies of government, as well as the attitudes of police forces, reflect their viewpoints. The President's National Advisory Commission on Civil Disorders declares, "The nation is rapidly moving toward two increasingly separate Americas . . . a white society principally located in suburbs . . . a Negro society largely concentrated within large central cities. . . ."[6]

The statistical and geographical facts are clear. In 1910, 91 per cent of American Negroes lived in the old South, most of them on plantations or in rural towns. By 1966 the Negro population had more than doubled and 68 per cent lived in metropolitan areas. Forty-five per cent of all Negroes now live outside of the old South and one-third of the total are concentrated in the nation's twelve largest cities, chiefly in their ghettos. Washington, D. C., and Newark, New Jersey, are already over half Negro.[7] If present trends continue through 1975, then New Orleans, Richmond, Baltimore, Jacksonville, Gary, and Cleveland will be more than 50 per cent black. If present trends persist through 1984, the same will be true of St. Louis, Detroit, Philadelphia, Oakland, and Chicago. As of 1968, one out of every five persons within the nation's central cities was a Negro. In the suburbs, the ratio was one out of twenty. Only one out of every fifteen Negroes now lives on a farm. In the context of American history, these are totally new demographic phenomena. Almost the entire black population of the country has been uprooted culturally, economically, and geographically from its rural past and set adrift amid indifferent or hostile urban whites who have blocked the main avenues of assimilation into the mainstream institutions of the metropolitan society.[8]

The President's Commission on Civil Disorders predicts that current trends toward an apartheid metropolitan society will continue unless they are offset by a genuine observance of civil rights, equal education-employment opportunities, and open housing. Furthermore, the Commission's report predicts that the growth of the U. S. white population between 1966 and 1975 will be 9.5 per cent while that of blacks will be 17.7 per cent.[9] It is the tendency of people who are not truly urbanized both culturally and economically to rely upon the agrarian system of social security, which is to have many children.

Black power and white backlash are part of the contemporary idiom. Psychologist Kenneth B. Clark cautioned a meeting of the Association of Existential Psychology and Psychiatry in New York that continued white violence aimed at keeping the Negro in second place was responsible for Negro uprisings and that this oppression indicates that the nation may be in a state of "terminal dry rot." Television shows us, Clark remarked, that there is a "relationship between the violence in Vietnam and in our cities." A wounded Negro veteran of the Vietnam fighting might have agreed. Upon his return to the ghetto to find it unchanged, he declared, "I'm ashamed of what I did in Vietnam. We did to yellow people what whites do to us."

After analyzing the Watts riot of 1965, the Los Angeles Police Department developed a comprehensive anti-riot plan which includes the concept called SWAT. At the request of the President's National Advisory Commission on Civil Disorders its outlines were published. "We have a SWAT team," explained Police Inspector Marton W. Howe, who is in charge of tactical operations planning for the Los Angeles Department. "That's our Special Weapons and Tactics team which breaks into four-man groups—a rifleman whose weapon has telescopic sights, a spotter and two officers with shotguns and hand guns to provide cover fire." By February, 1968, there were fifteen SWAT teams available to protect vital posts and operations, such as police stations or firemen and apparatus, that might become objects of snipers. Another thirty teams were being prepared.[10]

Major Robert A. Russell, who commanded sniper teams in Vietnam, is the author of a proposed 240-page Marine Corps manual. Major Russell thinks that it takes a superior man to be a superior rifleman. He must be highly intelligent, able to go for long periods without food or water, and able to control his emotions. "A sniper," says the author, "must kill deliberately, shooting carefully selected targets. . . . He must not be susceptible to emotions of anxiety or remorse." According to the Major, a potential sniper should pass a psychiatric screening test to make sure he has "certain essential mental qualities." Sniping, he notes, is a "very personal kind of fighting—you can see the look on people's faces" when they are shot. "The sniper," he declares, "must possess true equanimity, a perpetual self-possession and serenity which fosters maturity and patience." [11] Ideal characteristics, perhaps, for life in a socially polarized city.

Prosperity

Early in 1968 the United States completed its seventh year of uninterrupted economic growth. It had closed 1967 with a record gross national product of $763 billion. This meant goods and services totaling almost $3,800 for every man, woman, and child in the nation. No other country was even close to that figure. The day after *The New York Times* published these glad tidings, it reported that local police departments were buying armored riot control vehicles and stockpiling weapons. Richard McGlaughlin, sales manager for Smith & Wesson, revealed that sales to law enforcement agencies of guns, handcuffs, and tear gas "are at an all time high." The general manager of J. Tom Moore and Sons, makers of armored cars, declined to name the communities purchasing them. "It's ticklish business," he explained. "Everyone who has ordered cars has asked us not to disclose their names."

As riot control became big business, equipment makers prospered. The week of civil protests which followed the death of Martin Luther King produced a bull market for the stocks of companies in the "security industry." Bangor Punta Corporation, which controls Smith & Wesson, closed 22 per cent above its three-month low. The Breeze Corporation, whose subsidiary, Federal Laboratories, makes tear gas, grenades and projectiles, closed at 30⅜, up 72 per cent. Its low had been 17¾. Said William G. Gunn, president of Smith & Wesson, ". . . we feel that the equipment we're making is life saving equipment . . . we're selling all we can make." Commented President Joseph J. Mascuch of Breeze Corporation, "When this emergency happened, we ran out like water out of a barrel." The general public and institutional investors were confident that the shares of security and protection supply manufacturers were prime growth stock—making a strong contribution to a record gross national product in 1968. For the self-reliant citizen, corner drugstores in some cities began over-the-counter sales of "The Guardian"—a cigar-shaped spray weapon containing tear gas and retailing at $1.98. More than twenty companies are said to be making similar devices. One manufacturer which makes a deluxe spray weapon for $8 apiece reports sales of over one-quarter of a million of them.[12]

The build-up of police, National Guard, and Regular

Army arsenals in American cities was a major domestic goal of the Johnson Administration's final year. The conclusion of the President's National Advisory Commission on Civil Disorders was anticipated several months before its release. Officials knew its recommendations would run counter to their policy positions. Commitments to the Vietnam war and the federal spending they entailed precluded federal spending of a magnitude required to solve the urban crisis. The alternative and cheapest way out was to step up the police and choke off the protests.

Congressman William F. Ryan of New York described President Johnson's decision as a matter of priorities. "The commission's staff," said Ryan, "has reached the conclusion that vast sums of money must be expended to even make a dent on our impacted urban problem, and that this is viewed as politically inopportune. . . . The expenditure of $30 billion a year on war has created a climate where a Presidential commission must be muffled, lest it recommend a national effort of equal importance." [13]

By early spring, 1968, the Virginia State Police had bought six armored cars at $30,000 each. The sheriff of Los Angeles County had one and the police of Philadelphia and Detroit were trying to get two each. Chicago had bought three helicopters to use as observation posts during anticipated riots. Kansas City was under contract to purchase three specially equipped helicopters for round-the-clock police patrols. City officials had been induced to sign up for this equipment as the result of federally sponsored demonstrations of surveillance systems which showed that whirlybird teams can patrol areas fifteen times larger than ground units and do it better. Congress and the Executive Branch of the Federal Government were so pleased with helicopter performance that they agreed under the Crime Control and Safe Streets Act of 1968 to pay up to 75 per cent of the costs to establish local aerial police patrols or to improve existing programs. The new techniques were an unanticipated civilian bonus to come out of the Vietnam battlefields. Another was a national military-local police coordination central. A "hot line" telephone to the Pentagon was installed in Washington's City Hall and plans were drawn to merge the responses of police, National Guard, and Regular Army in case of civil disorders. It was a prototype for a nationwide network. Later a command post was established in the Pentagon to coordinate deployments of state and federal troops in every state. The Department of Justice collected data from cities across the nation to feed into a computer in its basement headquarters. The machine was expected to help prescribe the federal response at the outbreak of trouble. It was a battle plan for Operation American City. The rhetorical war against poverty and discrimination was to become a real one.

At Fort Gordon, Georgia, the Army conducted riot control seminars. It coached security forces from all over the country in the basic street tactics which later were demonstrated before the nation's TV audience as it watched the Chicago and Miami political conventions. Each week, beginning in February, a new class of police, guardsmen, and federal agents completed a twenty-hour course based on the grim lessons of the Detroit and Newark riots of 1967. Instruction included a demonstration of how a helicopter can swoop over a crowd, emit a cloud of tear gas, and blow it onto people below by the down-draft of its rotor blades. That particular technique eventually was unveiled with appalling effect to break up a student protest demonstration at the University of California at Berkeley. In a Hollywood-style mockup of an urban ghetto called "Riotsville" sham battles were conducted between a simulated troop of National Guardsmen and a mob of militant civil rights demonstrators led by a Negro sergeant named "Baby." As the mob waved signs denouncing war and proclaiming "We Shall Overcome," the guardsmen charged, using tear gas, bayonets, and an armored personnel carrier. "Baby" was grabbed and whisked away in the armored car.

In his State of the Union Address in January, President Johnson had said, "Today we are helping local officials improve their capacity to deal promptly with disorder. Those who preach disorder and violence must know that local authorities are able to resist them swiftly, sternly, and decisively." The President further promised to recommend legislation to encourage veterans from the fighting in Vietnam "to devote themselves to careers in community service." Major Russell's élite, possessing "true equanimity, a perpetual self-possession and serenity," was to be invited to employ its talents at home.

In the same State of the Union Address, President Johnson paid tribute to the national economy. "Americans are prosperous as men have never been in recorded history. Yet," he went on to observe, "there is in the land a certain restlessness —a questioning." Why, in a nation so incredibly rich in material resources, was there so little social resourcefulness? Without a positive response the restlessness and questioning would continue to escalate hand in hand with gross national product—obviously a socio-pathological absurdity.

Paradox

Contradictions and paradoxes, so conspicuous on the national scene, puzzle the rational minds of some young people. They want to know why, if technology is capable of abundance, society drags its feet; why, if it professes to be Christian, it is so uncharitable. The Gallup poll reports that 53 per cent of Americans want their churches to be silent on social issues. "The first duty of churches," they say, "is to comfort the individual." Others affirm that "Churches should concentrate on raising the levels of religious belief and practice." However, a majority of young people, age twenty-one to twenty-nine, think this is withdrawal from reality. According to the poll, they want an activist church to "express their views on

day-to-day social and political questions." They are not recon-
ciled to the idea of living in a polarized society.

The Bullet, student newspaper at Mary Washington College, Fredericksburg, Virginia, spoofed the notion that religion is to soothe individuals who want a reserved seat in
heaven rather than to disturb a smug society here and now.
A front page "mug shot" of Christ carried the alert: "WARN-
ING: this man is DANGEROUS—especially to the young . . .
a threat to your sons and daughters and the American way of
life." In typical "wanted" poster style, *The Bullet* explained
that Christ "urges followers to sell everything and give to
the poor . . . urges love, not war." Description: "typical hippie—beard, long hair, sandals, young . . . may be encountered
in any slum pad, love-in or antiwar demonstration." Dr.
Robert H. Shaw, pastor of Trinity Episcopal Church, was
scandalized. "Lousy journalism," he remarked. "I cannot see
any basis for all this concern with the general community."
"The most Christian thing we've ever done," proclaimed
editor Susan Wagner, a junior from Baltimore majoring in
American studies.[14]

A statistician for the National Council of Churches indicates that 10 million out of some 100 million church-goers
in the United States are actively opposed to church involvement in social issues. The majority, as indicated by the
Gallup poll, passively agrees with them. As they see it, the
job of religion and the church is to redeem souls, not to
redeem society. They view these ends as incompatible, even
contradictory. The Reverend Dr. Carl McIntire, president
of the International Council of Christian Churches, directs
a paid-time broadcast over 600 radio stations which de-
nounces ecumenism and social involvement while advocating
fundamentalist personal salvation. Kenneth Keyes, president
of Concerned Presbyterians, fears that arguments between
liberals and conservatives will split the denomination. He
believes that the control of most Protestant denominations
has fallen into the hands of "men who no longer believe that

the primary mission of the church is to lead the lost to Christ and to encourage believers to surrender themselves more fully and completely to Him." [15]

Professor Peter Berger of the New School for Social Research in New York informed a symposium in Rome sponsored by the Vatican Secretariat for Nonbelievers that middle-class youth is less interested in traditional religious consolations because childhood is happier now than formerly. Consequently, young adults who have had a sheltered childhood rebel when they move "into confrontation with less bliss-producing social structures of the adult world." They expect the institutions of the larger society beyond the family to be humane. When the happy fantasies of a protected middle-class childhood are shattered by the realities of a society that only professes to be religious while it practices ungodlike behavior, the inclination of the articulate college youth is not to climb back into the womb of myth but to challenge the adult world to drop its mask.

American religious organizations are a major industry with an estimated annual income from tax-deductible gifts alone of $6.5 billion. In the spring of 1969, black power leader James Forman started a national furor when he interrupted a service at Manhattan's fashionable Riverside Church to demand that churches and synagogues pay "reparations" of $500 million to black people who are treated unjustly by a society whose highest spiritual officeholders make no effective protest. When Mr. Forman began to read his statement, the Reverend Ernest T. Campbell, senior pastor of Riverside, promptly terminated the service, explaining afterward that he wanted to preserve the sanctity of worship. This explanation evoked the comment from Cannon Walter Dennis, a black Episcopalian on the staff of the Cathedral Church of St. John the Divine, that "Whenever a rite or ceremony is obscured and glorified for its own sake and is a form without commitment, it is a kind of profanity." Theologian Reinhold Niebuhr once observed that while individuals can relate to

each other on the basis of "purely moral and rational sua-
sion," the relations between groups are determined largely
by "the proportion of power which each group possesses."
If Niebuhr was right, therein lies the explanation of the
ability of confrontation politics to arouse the consciousness
if not the conscience of a complacent white society.

Priorities

Public agencies certified that 100,000 poor families in New
Jersey's Union and Hudson counties needed food supplements in July, 1968. At the time, 3,000 of them received
assistance through a Federal food stamp program which permitted the poor to buy $10 worth of food for $6. The 97,000
were eligible for stamps but they could not buy them. The
Federal Government refused to issue them. During the preceding fiscal year, July 1967-June 1968, some 3.3 million poor
people throughout the United States had received free surplus farm commodities worth $11 per month. Another 2.5
million obtained food stamp aid worth $6.73 per month. Sec-
retary of Agriculture Orville Freeman presented calculations
to Congress which indicated that there were an additional
17.5 million poor persons who would have been eligible for
food stamps but did not get them.

The stamps were withheld for two reasons. In the first
place, Congress appropriated only $185 million for a need
that the Secretary indicated would have required $1.5 bil-
lion. Secondly, the Department of Agriculture, operating
within these constraints, required local officials to request
stamps for the poor although Mr. Freeman had authority to
issue them without such requests. Since he was without funds
to give food to the poor, he gave them paperwork. Had Marie
Antoinette been as smart, she might have saved her head.

During the same fiscal year, the same Federal Department
of Agriculture issued checks for $4.5 billion to help farmers
all over the United States to stabilize their incomes. Most

of these funds were paid to farmers who agreed to cut back production of foods and fibers. The $4.5 billion was three times what it would have cost to let the U. S. hungry eat what they needed. Having studied the twin problems of hunger and surplus, the Department of Agriculture and the Congress decided that the best solution was to pay farmers not to raise the crops the poor could not afford to buy and to pay the farmers three times as much for not farming as it would have cost to let people eat who were not eating. Had she gone to Washington, Alice might have thought she was back in Wonderland.[16]

Most members of Congress liked Washington's farm programs—but not Representative Ray J. Madden of Indiana. He objected to paying farmers not to farm. He presented to the House in July, 1968, an itemized list of checks that had been sent out in 1967 by the Department of Agriculture to 407 cooperators to reward their tax-supported idleness. They ranged in amounts from a low of $101,040 to a top of $4,091,-818. There were five who got more than $1 million each; fifteen who got between $0.5 and $1.0 million. The rest got between $100,000 and $500,000. The $4,091,818 check that went to the J. G. Boswell Company of Kings County, Arizona, for not working, could have put the Government's food stamp program to work for one year for an additional 50,666 hungry people. The public cost of food stamp aid then averaged $80.76 per person per year. It was a question of priorities and political influence.

While a few colleagues agreed with Congressman Madden, the majority thought he was out of his mind. When these same facts were brought before the Senate in July, 1968, Senator John J. Williams of Delaware proposed that the Agricultural Act be amended to put a ceiling of $25,000 per year on all federal no-work welfare payments to big farmers. "If we want a program for the benefit of the small farmer," said Williams, "this amendment should be approved." It was defeated 47 to 25. Among those who voted it down was Farmer-

Senator James O. Eastland of Mississippi, whose corporation generally collects over $100,000 annually in Department of Agriculture welfare payments. In 1967 the Department of Agriculture presented Eastland Plantation Inc. with a no-work relief check for $157,930. No one in the Senate suggested a conflict of interest. In 1969 the House of Representatives finally voted 224 to 142 to set a limit of $20,000 on federal welfare payments to big farmers. The Senate Agriculture Committee, however, refused to go along with the idea. Instead, to show its sense of economy it rejected a proposal to give free food stamps to families with incomes of less than $40 a month. On the floor of the Senate the $20,000 ceiling was again proposed by Senator John J. Williams of Delaware but it was rejected 53 to 34. In Kansas twenty-nine counties had no food programs for the poor while their farmers got $4,274,533 in premiums for not producing food.

In 1968 when the farm subsidy program was being debated in the Congress, the *Chicago Tribune* noted that a prominent Mississippi farmer with 16,000 acres of land had been hauled into court and fined $50,000 for underpaying his 200 Negro tenants and for charging them $70 a month for shanties without inside water or plumbing when a "reasonable cost" would have been $5 a month. After his conviction for hiring child labor and paying adults less than the minimum $1.15 an hour Roy Flowers, the farmer, paid the fine "to get it out of court." Even so, he was still ahead of the game. In 1967, the Department of Agriculture had paid Flowers $210,-332 for idling some of his land. In 1966 it had paid him $162,647. Editorialized the *Tribune,* "Flowers may not be typical of plantation owners in the way he treats his hired help. But he is typical of a lot of big farmers and others who don't mind doing business with the government as long as it pays them huge sums at taxpayers' expense, but then squawk their heads off about 'government interference' when they get socked by a law they don't like." [17]

Who's Who

In 1935, American farms reached an all-time peak of 6.8 million units. It was then that federal agricultural programs really got under way. Now there are 2.9 million farms. The proportion of farmers in the American population dropped during the same years from 25 per cent to 5 per cent. As the little people dropped out, their land was bought up and consolidated by affluent survivors. In 1930, the average size of a farm was 157 acres. By 1964, it was 349 acres. Farms of over 1,000 acres or 1½ square miles accounted for 28 per cent of all agricultural land in 1930. By 1964, they accounted for 52.6 per cent.[18]

One result of big farms getting bigger while small ones disappear is that the top 4.5 per cent of all farms—the really big ones—now produce 42.6 per cent of all agricultural commodities. This is more food and fiber than is produced by the bottom 87.3 per cent, who accounted for 37.2 per cent of all farm output. These data are from the 1964 census of agriculture. When the 1969 census is published, it will probably reveal a greater disparity. As the number of farmers has declined, both the budget for the Department of Agriculture and the number of its employees have increased. From expenditures of less than $1 billion in 1935, the Department's outlays rose to $8.4 billion in fiscal 1969. Meanwhile, the number of its employees grew from less than 50,000 to over 100,000. In fiscal year 1967 the Department of Agriculture had 20 per cent more employees and a budget 22 per cent higher than it had had in 1960. During the same period, the farm population dropped 20 per cent.[19] The name of the game was Parkinson's Law.

Some years ago, when Senator Robert Griffin of Michigan was in the House of Representatives, he proposed to his colleagues that it be the sense of the Congress that at no time should the number of employees in the Department of Agriculture be permitted to exceed the number of farmers in the United States. His resolution was defeated.

Perhaps it was naive to expect federal officials to concern themselves with the poor and hungry since they do not have the expense accounts to lobby. Also they are stingy with campaign contributions, and they cannot afford to employ the law firms of senior Congressmen when jailed for demonstrating. It may be a paradox to young persons under thirty who have no nostalgic recollections of pre-war, small family-farmer America that the federal budget for 1969 gave the Department of Agriculture $8.4 billion to spend while the Department of Housing and Urban Development was allowed to spend $2.0 billion of the taxpayers' money.[20]

For Congressmen whose seniority on pivotal committees can make time stand still on Capitol Hill for at least thirty years, this is no puzzle. They legislate as though all the small farms that have disappeared since 1935 were still there just as they themselves are still there on the Hill. One reason the crisis of the city is so neglected is that Congress, which controls two-thirds of all America's tax wealth (federal, state, and local), still thinks with an agrarian mind.

Today's America is urban. That is where the action is—where the people are and where the future is being pounded out by the junior executive, the student activist, the stockbroker, the TV commentator, the dope-pusher, and the beautiful people. What Washington does for the big operators who have survived the agricultural revolution is irrelevant except for the public subsidies they get. What is relevant is what has happened to the farm dropouts, black and white, who are stuck in the urban slums—and the federal subsidies they do not get.

Like It Is

In 1961, New York's Columbia University leased 2.1 acres of nearby Morningside Park from the city administration of former Mayor Robert F. Wagner. The deal was approved by the Board of Estimate in October, 1967. The university, a private corporation, intended to build a gymnasium on the site. This arrangement, by which a piece of public park space in predominantly Negro Harlem was transferred to a university with a predominantly white student body, was resented by residents of the area. Black Harlem and white Columbia each had a different evaluation of Morningside Park.

Columbia claimed it was being generous to offer 16 per cent of the space in the new gymnasium to the black community for its use. Plans called for segregating that area and making it accessible from the street through a side entrance. The remaining 84 per cent was to be used separately by its own students. To Morningside's blacks and to some students it seemed that Columbia had flunked its own courses in sociology and city planning. It seemed to be caught with its academic hood down. It was a wheeler-dealer getting public property for its private use.

The Morningside gymnasium controversy, like a series of other campus incidents around the country, resulted in a confrontation between university students and their administration. The same world did not look the same to the programmers and those who were being programmed for the future.

In the spring of 1968, when Columbia's bulldozers moved into the park to level trees and prepare a site for the 11-million-dollar project a riot broke out. Students, faculty, and the black community demonstrated in unison against the university's president and its board of trustees. "It is not too late for Columbia to pull out," warned professor of architecture George R. Collins. "The university is getting itself into a position from which it should retreat." Columbia is one of the largest owners of slum real estate in the neighborhood around it. If it had needed land so badly it could have razed some of its own run-down properties, but rents from these were built into its projected budgets. The public park was a better deal.

Columbia did not pull out. As the gymnasium issue simmered other grievances surfaced and their protagonists took over the demonstrations. Students and faculty opposition to the draft and the Vietnam war flared up. While its deferred students were being reclassified 1A the university collaborated with the Institute for Defense Analyses on war-related research. Although its medical school had recognized the causal relationship between smoking and cancer the university accepted as a gift the controlling stock and royalty rights in a cigarette filter of questionable quality which it agreed to test and grade. On that issue Columbia surrendered and gave up its financial interests but the episode did not enhance its reputation for detached intellectual inquiry.

These and other issues eventually led to the siege and occupation of five campus buildings by student activists. President Grayson Kirk called in New York City's police to oust them. Rather than conduct a dialogue Manhattan's citadel of reason chose to use force. "The sight of blood," reported *The New York Times*, "of skulls cracked open, the screams, the sudden frightful face of violence in the protected and genteel enclave absolutely traumatized faculty and students alike." While the specific issues were different, repetitions of the Columbia confrontation between students and police had occurred the same year in Paris, Moscow, Shanghai, Prague, Caracas, Tokyo, London, and Mexico City. A new generation of young people was openly rebuking the hypocrisy of its elders who preached idealism but did not practice it. This slap in the face of duplicity was worldwide and it respected no political ideology because those ideologies were part of the hyprocrisy.

By the spring of 1969 dozens of other prestigious campuses had heard from their own rebellious students who declared that they were fed up with the indoctrination processes of the old order. Too many intellectuals, it appeared to them, were inclined to be apologists for things as they are rather than designers of what could be. Dr. James E. Allen, U. S. Commissioner of Education, suggested that trustees and officials of universities ought to take their protesting students seriously "and listen to them and treat them as adults." At a meeting of educators in New York, Stephen K. Bailey of Syracuse said of the current student generation: "The best of them are trying to tell us something." Mr. Bailey did not try to justify student disorders but he said they had a point. His own generation, he added, had not created all the world's ugliness and injustice but "we have perpetuated much of it, and we have been uncommonly slow to recognize and to ameliorate the most subtle indignities and tyrannies of our culture." [21]

All pretenses that higher education in America is intellectually detached ended when Harvard, the establishment's principal replenishment center, blew its cool on April 10, 1969. To bring a halt to a 17-hour occupation of University Hall staged by about 300 dissident students who wanted to talk, President Nathan M. Pusey and the Harvard administration requested police action. More than 400 helmeted state and local officers responded by wading in with clubs to smash heads in what later was called the most violent and divisive confrontation in Harvard's 330-year history. Reminiscing later a student whose arm was in a sling remarked, "They made no attempt to cope with the kind of non-violence we were using. . . . The people being clubbed reached up and tried to grab the policemen's sticks but failed to ward off the blows. Then I was sprayed with mace and ran into another room. I got this on my arm from trying to stop a cop from beating a girl who had two gashes on her head."

The students had rallied to protest the continued presence of Reserve Officers Training Corps units on their campus. It seemed to them that their university was being inconsistent by professing to solve problems with their minds while at the same time teaching them that violence is the ultimate argument. The police action that day in Harvard Yard indicated that Harvard's administration saw no such inconsistency.

Among the student protesters who were in University Hall on the day of the clubbing was Joseph Seamans, whose father was Secretary of the Air Force Robert C. Seamans.

As part of the aftermath of the campus riots Representative Dan Kuykendall of Tennessee proposed that federal aid be cut off to any university that does not make a "good faith" effort to quell student disturbances. He was joined by Ohio's Representative William H. Harsha, who wanted federal funds automatically suspended to any university at which there was a "substantial disruption." Senator J. W. Fulbright, himself a former professor, took a different view. In May, 1969, he delivered an indictment of "militarism" before the student body of the National War College, the élite of the Pentagon's young officers. Military policy, Senator Fulbright declared, has acquired an "inordinate" influence in the formulation of public policy with the result that the democratic values of American society are being "subverted." In foreign affairs he noted a trend to rely upon "the threat or the use of force. . . . Quite as inevitably as if it were deliberate," the Senator noted, "our imperial role in the world has generated a trend toward authoritarian government." The moral cost, he added, "is reflected in the unhappiness of the American people, most particularly in the angry alienation of our youth."

The Department of Defense, Senator Fulbright continued, "has become a vigorous partisan in our politics, exerting great influences on the President, on the military committees of the Congress, on the 'think tanks' and universities to which it parcels out lucrative research contracts, and on public opinion. . . . Every new weapons system or military installation soon acquires a constituency—a process which is aided and abetted by the perspicacity with which Pentagon officials award lucrative contracts and establish new plants and installations in the districts of influential members of Congress."

If some adults thought that the rebellious students who protested the draft and the training of professional militarists in institutions of higher learning were uninformed, perhaps they had not had time to reflect upon such matters as Senator Fulbright discussed before jumping to their conclusions. On the other hand they may have agreed with Governor Ronald Reagan of California, who proposed a resolution to the National Governors Conference in February of 1969 which declared in part, "Whereas disruptions on and around campuses throughout the nation have increased in number, in violence and in general disregard for the basic civilized values of our society. . . . Now therefore be it resolved that the Governors urge the President of the United States and the Department of Justice to authorize a full and complete investigation into the instigators, the causes and the effects of such violence which is no longer a series of isolated phenomena, but instead is nationwide. . . ." The governors rejected that particular resolution in favor of a milder one since Vice President Agnew had already assured them that the Justice Department, through the Federal Bureau of Investigation, was already watching. "As I understand it," Mr. Agnew told a news conference, "there is continuing activity in the Department of Justice in this area, not just when there are campus disturbances but routinely. They have an assignment to keep an eye on disturbances of this type." [22] Dissident students in Prague, Moscow, and Peking were also under surveillance by their own secret police.

While great campuses were in turmoil it remained for small but respected Amherst College to appeal to reason. For two days toward the end of April, 1969, all regular academic activities at Amherst were suspended while students, faculty, and administrators gathered for "debate, discussion and meditation" in their athletic field house. They openly expressed and examined their "beliefs about the nature of higher education and the governance of educational institutions." Several resolutions were adopted as well as a "student and faculty Bill of Rights." As a final act it was decided that a letter should be drafted by their president, Calvin H. Plimpton, to President Richard Nixon "expressing Amherst's concern for the relationship between the crisis on college campuses and the larger crisis in America."

The brief document that resulted produced light where an exacerbating exchange of recriminations had all but usurped the field. The letter from president to president said in part, "Institutions dedicated to the nurture, husbanding, and growth of critical intelligence, and to inquiry into basic problems cannot but open people's eyes to the shoddiness of many aspects of our society. In yesterday's [May 1] *New York Times* it is reported that five officers in your Cabinet seemed to agree that the disorder was caused by a small minority of students. Our conviction is that such a view is seriously in error if it is taken to mean that no legitimate and important reasons exist for the anger and sense of impotence felt by many students and faculty. The pervasive and insistent disquiet on many campuses throughout the nation indicates that unrest results, not from a conspiracy by a few, but from a shared sense that the nation has no adequate plans for meeting the crises of our society. To name only one issue of special concern to the students: since the Kerner Commission's [President's National Advisory Commission on Civil Disorders] report, there has been no decisive response to its recommendations. We do not say that all the problems faced by colleges and universities are a reflection of the malaise of the larger society. That is not true. But we do say that until political leadership addresses itself to the major problems of our society—the huge expenditure of natural resources for military purposes, the inequities practiced by the present draft system, the critical needs of America's 23,000,000 poor, the unequal division of our life on racial issues—until this happens, the concern and energy of those who know the need for change will seek outlets for their frustration. . . ." [23]

"The ferment of youth is potentially of enormous benefit to society," says John D. Rockefeller 3rd, chairman of the Rockefeller Foundation. He observes that "young people today learn faster and mature earlier. They become quickly aware—and deeply resentful—of the differences between what older people say and what they do. In short, the very accomplishments of our generation—in technology, communication, affluence—have served to focus the attention of the young on what we have failed to accomplish." Rockefeller cites a VISTA slogan which, he says, captures this spirit: "If you're not part of the solution, you're part of the problem." [24] Universities, which for so long have thought of themselves as "the solution," are now finding that they are a part of the problem.

As a customer in the cafeteria of knowledge the college student is expected to pick a balanced diet from the many dishes on display. It is up to him to correlate what the university faculty in its departmentally specialized autonomy does not organize. He is expected to learn what he is not taught. He is expected to synthesize while he is taught to specialize. He must generalize what has been atomized. As he samples here and there he wonders what it all adds up to. There is a correlation gap—a surplus of facts and a shortage of unifying concepts. If he is bright his intuition impels him to ask questions. He learns that the pure economist is concerned with the growth of gross national product, not with social consequences. The sociologist, he finds, may be content to research things as they are and say, "That's it." When he learns from physics and engineering about the dynamics of modern technology he wonders why social scientists can be so complacent. When he learns from anthropologists about his own culture and from psychologists about the human mind, he wonders if they are not capable of more devastation than atomic fission and what should be done to prevent a blowup.

Why should university students, who obviously are designated to be among the future élite, question the behavior of those who hold equivalent privileges now? Are they not in fact jeopardizing their own prospects? Why should they protest against any system, whatever its political ideology, which promises them special responsibilities, powers, and rewards? For one thing not all students protest. Only a minority gets aroused although it is reported that those who do are among the brightest, most articulate, and aware. Perhaps that explains it. Those who have taken their educations seriously come to see quite clearly the contradictions between social folklore and social behavior that remain obscure to others. These contradictions between rhetoric and reality never before have been so numerous or so unacceptable. In no previous age did there actually exist a genuine potential for total human well-being such as science and technology now provide. At the same time achievement of the potential is stymied by a carryover from the past of obsolete social rigidities based on the rationale of scarcity.

The bright student sees the welfare of all mankind being sidetracked by the selfishness of the privileged, whether they are a minority upper crust as in India, a majority white middle class as in America, or a bureaucracy of politically certified technocrats as in the Soviet Union. The college student who takes his courses seriously learns things that, because of their irrationality, would puzzle any rational mind. He finds that universities, far from looking at the world universally, comprehensively, and interrelatedly, are the incubators of specialization, of the detailed look at the small field. They put the knowledge of science and engineering in distinctively marked packages so that it will not get mixed up with those packages that contain the knowledge of social sciences and humanities. Faculties, once they have decided upon their specialties, are expected to concentrate on them. Curriculum committees, mindful of vested interests, object to professorial trespassing. An instructor must stick to his own bailiwick and not get involved in the concerns of other disciplines. He belongs to an intellectual union and must not cross picket lines.

As he looks around for himself this student discovers that what could be a reasonable, sensible, rather decent society is deeply bogged down in contradictions between what it is and what it pretends to be. Grown men in the world's most powerful positions play games with the gullible. If the sickness of cities is ever to be cured—and the sickness is worldwide—there will have to be a change in national priorities from force to reason. In America the city, not the farm, will have to be recognized as the national environment—limited not by the scarcities of nature but only by a failure to use intelligence and vision.

Perception

Physicists tell us that any resemblance between the real world and the world we perceive with our senses is unlikely. We see, feel, hear, and smell only what our sensory equipment permits us to be aware of. We know from what the congenitally blind report that their environment is full of sounds and smells most if us do not notice. We in turn tell them of sights which they can only imagine. If we were electronic meters instead of people we would find ourselves in the midst of an omnidirectional bombardment of high-frequency radiation undetectable by human senses. If we were electron microscopes solids would be lattices composed mostly of nothing.

Our human senses give us awareness of a universe that suits them. Fortunately they do not report what they cannot detect. Otherwise we might be listening to the cross fire of a thousand simultaneous but different radio and TV programs with no way to tune out. We know from the instruments science has invented that "things are not what they seem" but we function as though they were because our nervous systems are rigged to respond instinctively to what we are programmed to notice rather than to what is.

To make matters more confusing psychologists inform us that no two persons react equally to the same experience—not because our equipment differs but because each of us perceives in terms of past experiences. The greater the divergence in background the greater likelihood of divergent responses to the same stimuli. A Wall Street broker and a Harlem Negro react differently to a helmeted white police officer. We have no other way of knowing ourselves, our society, or the universe except what experience has conditioned us to know. As specialization increases in an advanced urban society there is a multiplication of the ways in which individuals are programmed by experience. Contradictions between views, attitudes, convictions, and assumptions increase. Communications break down. Agreement becomes more difficult. Even the most prestigious institutions of the intellect fail.

In Australia 300 school children were told by a teacher about the Javas—a race whose homeland was identified as Queen Island to the northwest in the Pacific Ocean. The Javas, it was reported, differ from Australians physically and wear veils to hide their faces. The children learned that these odd people sleep by day while at night they move about stealthily. They relish the flesh of young calves, which they kill by slitting their throats and letting the blood drain out. As the children became more familiar with Java lore they began to hate and fear those people whom they had never before seen or heard of. At the conclusion of the study, after their passions had been aroused, the teacher informed them that the Javas of Queen Island were fictitious.

3

Toward a Theory of the City

In science, theory is used when truth is elusive. A metaphysical effort is made to relate phenomena so that order displaces chaos. The human mind is uncomfortable with chaos. It is uncomfortable with cities as they are, and it is in search of some workable theory that will make them more manageable and more livable. Is a theory of the city possible?

Hot Water

French sociologist Michel Crozier raised a storm in Europe when he praised the ability of American industry to organize science and technology for more efficient production. Angry Europeans interpreted this compliment to U. S. business management as an endorsement of the Americanization of European society. Nothing could have appalled M. Crozier more. He sees clearly the distinction between the management of technology and the management of society. He does not think highly of the way society is institutionalized either in America or in Europe. Present social structures, he says, "in France and other European countries are not flexible enough to enhance the role of the individual, and if we just waited for scientific miracles, we would come back to the same arrogance of rationality one criticizes in the United States." [1]

When M. Crozier came to the United States in 1968 to address a meeting of ninety intellectuals from twenty countries he got into an argument with American eggheads who, he declared, are in danger of "becoming as overextended in their intellectual resources as their country has become overextended in its political commitments in the world." American arrogance, M. Crozier believes, arises from the assumption that advanced "social engineering" can steer mankind into an era of peace and plenty by the rational methods of scientific technology—just discover the right methodology and apply it, and it will print out answers to the world's social problems. *Sacre Dieu,* what gross oversimplification! "It means to be blind to cultural and institutional diversity. . . . It is a kind of folly," M. Crozier contends, to assume that "a rational view of the world based on the inevitability of scientific progress can cope with a fragmented, culturally diverse society full of complex emotional problems. . . . Techniques must be applied within the context of humanist perspective." [2] Now Michel Crozier is in hot water on both sides of the Atlantic. But he should be a happy marksman. He scored two direct hits.

A New Ecology

The most significant characteristic of modern urbanization is that it creates a new *ecological system.* It is first of all a biological phenomenon, but it has become distinctly so just recently. Even now this is true only of our one-third of the world, which has reached a stage of advanced urbanization. With us the city has replaced the age-old ecological reciprocation between man and nature which prevailed in the rain forest and on the farm. With us natural man and the natural environment are passing into extinction and will survive as curiosities only if deliberately protected.

By urbanizing, man shifts his dependence from what nature makes to what he intentionally creates and protects. The results may be good or bad, safe or dangerous, beautiful or ugly, clean or polluted depending upon how the job is done. Nature, luck, and tradition no longer have anything to do with our fortunes as a society now that we have created our own synthetic environment and have in turn become reliant upon it. We could not survive without it. It is also possible that we will not survive because of it.

Man as a distinct genus has been on earth for perhaps a million years. It took him 99 per cent of that time just to get ahead of other living species which might have done him in. From the beginning our progenitors had superior brains but they lacked information. That was picked up slowly, experimentally. Meanwhile they were handicapped. They were not the fastest runners. They did not have the longest claws or the sharpest teeth. Each new invention from the throwing stick to the plow increased their chances of survival. The inventions of agriculture and animal husbandry made possible the man-land ecology of preurban societies. It was the culminating achievement of prehistory.

Growing out of this interdependence of man and land—man cultivated the land; the land supported him—were new social systems, new mechanical technologies, fixed communities, primitive modes of transportation and trade. Most important of all were the customs, beliefs, and value codes which oriented the minds of individuals so that they came to function as coherent societies. Since technological change was slow so was change in customs, beliefs, and values. Groups which shared techniques and thought processes were insulated from others by the barriers of language and geography. In those days the world was big and made of innumerable small parts. Diversities in culture developed but cultural friction was minimized as long as societies kept within their boundaries. Friction is an interface phenomenon.

By urbanizing modern man took a giant step. The small

parts began to interconnect as he shifted his security from the natural landscape to the synthetic environment deliberately created. Materially the city is an astonishing success. Its techniques ramify the usability of nature's resources—allow us to do more with less. But there remains one serious deficiency. As an urban creature man has not yet developed the customs, beliefs, and value codes that condition him to live coherently as a larger, heterogeneous society. This task is complicated and valved by the fact that, while we are fast becoming one world technologically, we remain socially and politically fractionated. We have been conditioned by our agrarian heritage to live peacefully in small groups whose members are psychologically programmed by traditional cultures to respect the values of their respective groups. We do well as homogeneous fractions. We have not learned to be a heterogeneous whole. We are psychologically unprepared for urbanization, which calls for concentration of diverse culture groups within the confined spaces of cities. By driving toward a world econo-technic system urbanization is also pushing for a compatible world society.

As technological integration weaves the world together into a common resource-generating network it forces clashes between culture groups. The evidence is everywhere. These clashes occur not only between nations but also within nations which are culturally diverse. The United States, because of its extraordinary cultural diversity and speed of its urbanization, is having a particularly rough time. We are a multiply interfaced society with high friction probability.

What Europe calls the arrogance of Americanization—the push toward an integrated world econo-technic system—provokes social change and this is resented. And nowhere are the pressures for social adjustment to technological rationalization more resented than in America itself. We are an ethnically, regionally, religiously, racially, and economically segregated society, yet as an advanced urban system we are subject to the most powerful technological influences to integrate. We are obviously suffering from environmentally induced social schizophrenia.

Theoretically one way to resolve cultural differences would be to homogenize the cultures or encourage one to dominate all others. This is what Michel Crozier would resist. It is what most people would object to. Unless they were members of the aggressive society, already psychologically conditioned to accept its values, people would resent the superposition of another culture upon their own. Such an overlay could threaten everything they regard as wonderful and holy. To homogenize all cultures by mixing them into a blend would confuse everyone—it would sterilize the individual mind and put all humanity in a psychological straitjacket. The alternative to homogenization is the acceptance, toleration, and appreciation of cultural diversity in the broadest sense. Such acceptance, toleration, and appreciation would have to be developed in our stimulus-response mechanisms from earliest childhood.

Because urbanization calls for the concentration of populations and increases the frequencies of their interactions, nationally and worldwide the need grows for new social institutions and customs which will encourage respect and appreciation for cultural diversity—which will allow every culture group to do its own thing. As the technological imperative of efficiency tends to coordinate all peoples into a universal resource-producing system the need increases for a society that respects man's psychic well-being and cultural heterogeneity. This is the most critical task of the synthetic environment, which already possesses the blueprints for satisfying material needs. Obviously such a goal could not be achieved by groups that would substitute institutional segregation for geographic segregation. Social apartheidism is an agrarian anachronism in a technologically interconnected urban environment.

Crowding

Urbanization is a crowding process diametrically contrary to the dispersals of paleolithic hunters and neolithic farmers. It is a concentration phenomenon that gains in scale and density because it is technologically feasible. There is no proof that it is biologically desirable. In fact, as urbanization has evolved to date, there is evidence that it is both physiologically and psychologically dangerous. More resources are produced but the punishment we take to produce them is severe. The life span is extended but life quality is threatened. Leisure is increased; so is psychosomatic illness.

The physician A. T. W. Simeons contends that psychosomatic disorders ranging from peptic ulcers to coronary disease originate because the body is caught in a conflict of commands issued by separate parts of its own brain. Our conscious, rationalizing cerebral cortex, a recent product of evolution, insists under social compulsion that it overrule and suppress more primitive instinctual instructions of the brain stem which we have inherited from prehumanoid vertebrate ancestors. The consequence of these mixed-up commands is a long list of visceral, nervous, muscular, and bone malfunctions that are attributable to our urbanized existence. Far from being soft, city life produces tensions and stresses for which our physiological evolution did not prepare us. In establishing a new ecology we have created an environment incompatible with our natures. But it is not the physical shell that is basically at fault. Rather it is our culture, of which the architectural envelope is simply a by-product.

The city, of course, is a cortical invention. If what Simeons is saying is valid, then its cultural evolution should be more respectful of our physiological nature. Conventional codes of behavior are safety devices. If they are to work rather than create havoc they must apply equitably. They should not restrict freedoms unless the safety of others is endangered. The constraints for everyone should be the same. Every member of the community should have ample opportunity both to acquire the skills which can make him viable and to develop a personality structure that would result in adaptive behavior. Any hypocrisy such as the establishment of double standards of compliance with culture norms would be certain to frustrate individuals and preclude healthy social interaction. This is a tall order, for it imposes upon society an obligation to be just as fair to the individual as the individual is expected to be toward society. An unjust society can expect violence. In fact violence may be considered the mark of an unjust society.

Psychologist Ernest Haggard studied the effects of crowding upon men confined in submarines. "Some of the factors which influence an individual's ability to tolerate and master stress," he reports, "include: the nature of his early identifications and his present character structure, and their relation to the demands and gratifications of the present stress-producing situation . . . his ability to master strong and disturbing emotional tensions . . . so that he is not helplessly unaware of the nature and source of threat . . . his available skills and . . . the strength and pattern of his motivations to do so." [3]

Looking at people confined to slums and ghettos may not be comparable to studying men in submarines, but the question might be raised appropriately as to what preparation they get from infancy by way of family or neighborhood experience that would enable them to develop the "character structure" or "identification patterns" that would prepare them for adaptive behavior in the city at large. What encouragement or successes have they had that would develop a sense of mastery over strong and disturbing emotional tensions? As an ecological system the city must provide more than a shell of buildings and streets. It must provide more than material resources; it must be humane.

Few detailed studies of the mental health of civilian populations have been made. One of the more elaborate was conducted a few years ago by a team of social scientists and psychiatrists under the direction of Thomas A. C. Rennie, M. D., of Cornell University Medical College. It included a home interview survey of 1,660 persons, aged twenty to fifty-nine, who were living in midtown Manhattan—a substantial middle-class neighborhood. Psychiatrists thought 18.5 per cent of them were free of all but inconsequential symptoms of mental illness. A total of 58.1 per cent showed mild to moderate symptom formation. There were 20.7 per cent with marked to severe symptom formation. Two and seven-tenths per cent were incapacitated by mental illness. Persons with marked symptom formation or worse were all regarded as being mentally impaired. Of the 23.4 per cent of the Cornell sample who thus were handicapped four out of five had never had treatment for their illness. The Cornell data further revealed that persons in the highest socioeconomic stratum had the highest rate of mental health. Only 12.5 per cent were impaired while 30.0 per cent were well. In the lowest socioeconomic stratum 4.6 per cent were well and 47.3 per cent were impaired.[4] This was the situation in one of New York's better neighborhoods.

Social historian Jacques Ellul finds that modern urban man has started an environment-making process which, unless deliberately regulated and guided by astute insights, will within a short time produce a habitat hostile to his welfare. Technology, as Ellul defines it, is organizational as well as mechanical. To accommodate mass populations in modern urban densities calls for elaborate specialized operations and the closest synchronization of these operations. Interactions become so intricate, yet interdependent, that the entire process tends to dominate men rather than men the process. This is the ultimate crowding of the individual into a system of conformity that deprives him of a sense of self. Denied self-respect, the individual retaliates by reacting with contempt for society.

How much crowding can a living organism endure without elaborate safeguards being taken to preserve integrity? Working with confined populations of domesticated Norway rats, John B. Calhoun of the National Institute of Health found that as numbers increased and space remained constant the rats reached a state of sustained inordinate aggregation which he called "pathological togetherness" because it led to a number of serious aberrations in behavior, organic malfunctions, and death. Females failed to follow through with nest burrows. In transferring young from one hiding place to another mothers would drop some midway, turn to some other activity and leave their offspring to be eaten by other rats. In their sexual manifestations males dispensed with normal ritual and rushed females without invitation. Some mounted other males and juveniles of both sexes. Aggressive males bit adults and young of both sexes. Some pregnant females aborted. Others died and upon autopsy were found with partially resorbed embryos. Calhoun drew no inferences about human beings from his study of the Norway rat but one wonders if mankind is risking "pathological togetherness" by permitting high densities to occur without having reached a higher plane of cultural sophistication.[5] Results similar to those of Calhoun's were obtained independently by Dr. Kurt Richter at the Johns Hopkins University.[6]

With respect to man, animal behaviorist Konrad Lorenz notes that "it is quite possible that a cultural tradition of behavioral norms originated as early as the use of tools or even earlier. The beginnings of both have been found in the chimpanzee." [7] These behavioral norms give cohesion to groups. They are proved ways of dealing successfully with environmental stresses both physical and social. They inform us subconsciously, instinctively, of the character and intent of one another's attitudes and actions. They are in truth "codes." Members of the group know the code, observe its rituals. Strangers may not. To get signals mixed, to misinterpret the code, or violate custom is to raise an alarm; cause

fear and suspicion; invite risks. Thus it is a threat to anyone or any group when its culture is challenged. It is a survival mechanism. Segregated culture groups living in physical proximity in an urban environment can expect conflict
because segregation prevents each from learning the other's
behavioral codes.

Lorenz observes that "the extreme speed of ecological and
sociological change wrought by the development of technology causes many customs to become maladaptive within one
generation." And to make things worse, "scientific enlightenment tends to engender doubt in the value of traditional
beliefs long before it furnishes the causal insight necessary
to decide whether some accepted custom is an obsolete super-
stition or a still indispensable part of a system of social
norms." He concludes that "it usually proves highly dangerous to mix cultures" because there is a balanced interaction
between all the single norms of social behavior characteristic
of a culture." [8] Science and technology have enabled modern
man to urbanize his way of life and they have given him the
capacity to create energy and resources. The task remaining
is to develop a culture that is responsive to change when the
character of culture as we now know it is to help us adapt to
things as they are. Of course all cultures evolve just as environments do but now the process must be accelerated because technology is changing the environment so rapidly.

Dr. August F. Kinzel, a professor of psychiatry at Columbia University's College of Physicians and Surgeons, has conducted experiments which indicate that people may differ
considerably in their responses to crowding. As subjects he
used two classes of prisoners: those who were convicted of
crimes of violence against persons and those who were guilty
of crimes against property. Each individual was placed in
the middle of a small, bare room; then he was approached
slowly by Dr. Kinzel. The "body buffer zone" or area within
which the subject felt secure from Dr. Kinzel's intrusion, was
found to be four times larger among those who had mani-

fested violence than among those who had not. "Mispercep-
tions of the experimenter as 'looming' or 'rushing' at the
subjects, were reported frequently by the violent subjects,"
Dr. Kinzel related. "By contrast, the non-violent group let
the experimenter approach closer than ordinary conversa-
tional distances and did not report 'looming' or 'rushing'
sensations." Dr. Kinzel does not know what triggers the un-
easiness of some persons at the approach of others but it is
thought that his experiments may provide a possible explanation for the greater incidence of crimes of violence in slums
than in less crowded places where persons with short proximity fuses are less frequently set off.[9]

Life in big cities produces "deindividuation" according to
Dr. Philip G. Zimbardo, professor of psychology at Stanford
University. Deindividuation, he explains, is the dissolution
of the self-imposed restraints upon deviant behavior that are
commonly exercised by members of large families or small
communities. "What we are observing around us, then," says
Dr. Zimbardo, "is a sudden change in the restraints which
normally control the expression of our drives, impulses and
emotions." The sheer size of many cities, the feeling of power-
lessness in the face of big institutions, the widespread renting
of apartments rather than the owning of houses, and the high
mobility of our populations are among the factors to which
Dr. Zimbardo attributes a weakening of self-applied behavioral controls based on self-evaluation. Manifestations of
deindividuation range from increases in vandalism to riots
and murder. He notes that in 1967 in New York alone
202,712 school windows and 360,000 pay telephones were
smashed. "Conditions which foster deindividuation," Dr.
Zimbardo says, "make each of us a potential assassin." [10]

Anxieties, frustrations, and cold sweats resulting from close
crowding among the unfamiliar are not the sole prerogative
of crowded slum dwellers. Newcomers to Congress and Washington's executive departments also feel uncomfortable in
social situations to which they are unaccustomed. To put

them at ease a special school in the nation's capital teaches them table manners, including how to fold a napkin and the proper technique for attacking crêpe suzettes. They learn how to select a good wine, and to arrange flowers. Well drilled in proper etiquette graduates find themselves able to attend $1,000-a-plate political suppers without suffering from "culture shock."

In the spring of 1969 Washington's prestigious Smithsonian Institution held an international conference on "Man and Beast: Comparative Social Behavior." At one of the final sessions social psychologist Robert B. Zajonc of the University of Michigan said that his own research indicates both man and animals like what they like because it is familiar. One's capacity for attachment he says "consists simply of one's capacity to gain love through exposure." Professor Zajonc's conclusions rebut the old idea that like likes like because it is like. "The mere repeated exposure of an individual to a given stimulus object," he says, "is a sufficient condition for the enhancement of his attitude toward it, be this stimulus object a member of the same species, of different species, or an inanimate object." Lambs he found would just as soon love a television set as their own mother if they are isolated from other stimuli. In one of his experiments with rats he found that those exposed in early life to the music of either Mozart or Schoenberg show a strong liking in later life for other music by the composer they were raised on, and reject the composer unfamiliar to them. "Each species and each aggregation has probably its own particular equilibrium whereby the tendencies to approach and become attached are restrained by their opposites." [11]

For lack of a common culture to relate them American urban whites feel threatened by the increasing ratio of blacks to whites in central cities. Thus the flight to suburbia of middle-class whites could be viewed as a maneuver to preserve their cultural identity and thereby appease an instinctive fear that they are threatened by the unfamiliar. A growing acceptance of the black power mystique among Negroes results from a conscious effort by the articulate leaders to develop genuine cultural coherence among a people who, previously fragmented and denied acceptance by the larger society, have been highly vulnerable—commonly exploited and sometimes murdered with impunity. The development of black power culture is, therefore, also a survival technique.

A nation which neglects to develop a culture that interrelates all its components by making allowances for subcultural variety must expect to become a split society as its segregated components stress both their internal similarities and their differences from others. Cultural differences intensify as the consequence of both geographic and institutional segregation. At the interfaces of contact friction then increases. By ignoring such basic biological characteristics of man as a social animal the astonishing material advantages of our late twentieth-century industrial technology are being dissipated. What we have gained by harnessing inanimate nature with material technology has been depreciated by our failure to face up to the imperatives of human nature by developing a more humane society.

Historically

Historians and the ancient chroniclers tell us that Greek and Roman cities, in their beginnings, did not happen by chance. They were deliberately preplanned and socially preorganized before coming into existence. From Fustel de Coulanges we learn that "With the ancients, a city was never formed by degrees, by the slow increase of the number of men and houses. They founded a city at once, all entire in a day; but the elements of the city needed to be first ready, and this was the most difficult, and ordinarily the largest work. As soon as the families, the phratries, and the tribes had agreed to unite and have the same worship, they immediately founded the city as a sanctuary for this common worship, and thus the foundation of a city was always a religious act." Cities in those days were more like rural villages—chiefly inhabited by farmer families who cultivated the surrounding lands. The building of physical shells of structures and landscapes followed the formation of coherent culture groups. Today we build such architectural shells for the cohabitation of culturally unreconciled groups.

When families and tribes confederated to form a new city they brought into it with them their gods, sacred fires, and a reverence for private property. All three were interrelated and necessary to provide food, shelter, and security—the primary environmental prerequisites of any living organism. "In the house of every Greek and Roman was an altar; on this altar there had always to be a small quantity of ashes, and a few lighted coals." Fustel de Coulanges tells us that this perpetual fire was believed to be the spirit of the family's gods, who were its departed ancestors. During the agrarian period of human association the dead were buried on some reserved quarter of the family's cultivated ground. Vestigial forms of this association of spiritual fires, worship of the ancestral dead, and regard for the family's land are still to be observed in such widely separated places as rural Japan and some Mayan Indian communities in Guatemala.[12]

By burying the immortal dead upon their own soil, the living assured themselves of supernatural aid. As long as sacred fires were kept, the ancestral spirits dwelt among them to protect them and make their fields productive. For an agrarian people, it made sense that private lands should have both a temporal and religious significance. That real estate sustained them in this life and gave them a place and an identity in the hereafter.

Until the evolution of the industrial metropolis, which relies for its resources upon intelligence and inanimate energy, private property remained the most important basis of family income and security. It is powerfully respected by all legal systems derived from Roman law. Even in the contemporary city, it is still custom to associate family security with property although now that protection in most cases rests upon employable talent. So powerful are conventional patterns of thought that even after technology has transformed the mechanics of life, old cultural beliefs, customs, and values are carried over into the subsequent environment. As such, they become mental blocks to new ways of thinking that might be more appropriate to the new context. Urbanization encourages a culture more respectful of resource-producing talents than of resource-producing property. It, therefore, conflicts with a fundamental precept of agrarian societies.

When Herman Miller made his statistical analysis of income distributions in the United States, he found that even among the top 5 per cent property was a minor factor in their earnings. "If you believe that there are large numbers in this top group who make their living by clipping coupons, you couldn't be farther from the truth." Miller writes, "In 1960, only one family out of a hundred in the top 5 per cent lived entirely on unearned income—interest, dividends, rents, royalties, and the like. The other ninety-nine did paid work or were self-employed. . . . The great majority of families in the top 5 per cent income group are there because they are headed by a man whose skills are much in demand and who therefore has high earning potential." [13]

While some ideals of vanishing agrarian societies still have their urban protagonists, the allegiance is more verbal than real. Self-sufficiency and hard physical labor are still said to be virtues but today's winners are not hung up on them. To play the rugged individualist would be the quickest way to be taken for some kind of nut in our organization-man society. Willingness to do hard physical labor is practically indicative of mental illness. The hardest kind of physical labor in the United States is performed by the landless farm worker. In 1966 there were 1.6 million adult farm workers over twenty years of age. Fifty-one per cent of them earned between $3 and $9 a day. Twenty-seven per cent earned from

$9 to $13 a day. Sixteen per cent earned over $13 a day while six per cent earned less than $3 a day.

So many contemporary values and beliefs are carryovers from our agrarian past that to mouth them while not practicing them produces the contradictions between ideals and realities that everywhere are so evident in our society—which provoke the young to cry hypocrisy at the inconsistencies of their elders. The city has really come into existence as America's dominant environment within the lifetime of the present older generation. Yet that generation holds great institutional power, particularly in government, where seldom is there an obligatory retirement age for those in the most prestigious positions. Politically, urban policy is still being made with agrarian minds.

As recently as 1920 the population of the United States was half urban and half rural. Most conventional thinking is still more in tune with a rural than with the urban environment. It is impossible, therefore, to formulate a workable theory of the city without beginning with some appraisal of the agrarian mind. It is that mind, with its carryover of obsolete concepts and values, which is the primary obstacle to the evolution of an urban environment that could be ecologically appropriate.

The Agrarian Mind

Two ecologies so radically different as the agrarian and the urban could be expected to generate equally distinct philosophies of life and society. Given time each would generate a different culture with different beliefs, customs, and standards of values. The farmer who believes in self-sufficiency ridicules the interdependence of urban organization-man. The supremacy of property rights conflicts with a supremacy of human rights. The fence and the wall around private lands are the antithesis of the open public square, public park, and public beach. Government services based upon the taxation of land as the primary social asset have an entirely different rationale from government services based on levies against talents via the income tax. The rights of localities versus the rights of larger communities, states, and the nation are appraised differently by the agrarian and the urbanite.

Since responsibilities are the consequence of rights in a civilized society they, too, are evaluated differently by townsman and countryman. First and foremost to the true agrarian is the sacred character of his land, which is local, immediate, and tangible. The strongest government from the standpoint of taxation and public services should therefore be local. The relationship between his private land and public government should be as intimate as their geographic proximity. All else is secondary. All else of a social nature derives from that. His concept of law, order, and justice, his sense of responsibility to the community and of the community to him, his notions of public service and social welfare—all are tied to the function of land as distinct from the function of talent.

The farmer's world is a world of acres, limited in area, limited in productivity. It is a world of limits in which scarcity is the consequence of too many people and too little space to go around. It is a society that honors competition for property because it is scarce and fixed and therefore serves as a symbol and measure of status, ability, and character. Above all it is the essence of security. The agrarian believes in scarcity because scarcity becomes real in the natural environment as soon as populations grow numerous and there is not enough land to go around. Because land is visible and tangible the agrarian is particularly attuned to the concrete and specific which are directly sensed by eyes, ears, nose, and touch. The weightless, invisible, untouchable, odorless, noiseless universe of abstract thought responsible for modern science and technology is largely beyond his perception and scarcely enters his calculations.

An ecological theory of the city might begin with two hypotheses: (1) that the function of any environment is to make it possible for the inhabitant to secure food, shelter, and security; (2) that the function of any society is to include the individual.

In an agrarian environment the extent and productivity of the land determines how many people can be supported and how well. The Jeffersonian ideal of the good society based upon farming envisioned enough land so that everyone who chose to be a husbandman could have a homestead to support his family. With his own property which he and his family could cultivate, Thomas Jefferson believed the farmer would be economically secure and thus politically independent. The result—a virtuous and democratic people. The purchase of the Louisiana Territory, it was hoped, would not only remove France from young America's rear doorstep but would also provide homesteads for all who might apply. Ecologically the ideal agrarian environment could be diagrammed as a landscape of farms, each with a fence around its boundaries, and each with land enough to give employment to the family so that it might support itself. Diagram 1 expresses the idea: four homesteads, surrounded by land, surrounded by fences.

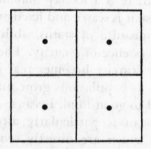

For such a society of freeholders to survive, government should not tax heavily, for otherwise the land might be put in jeopardy and thus the whole institutional structure would be threatened. With income dependent upon manual labor and animal power little surplus could be generated. The government which governed least was certainly best. Thus local government was held to be the most democratic, for it was close at hand and could be most easily restrained by the landholding electorate. (It is still the custom in New England towns to permit only property holders to vote at the annual financial meeting.) There was no need for heavy public expenditures according to the agrarian ethic. Each family was responsible for building and maintaining its portion of the road to market. Education was rudimentary. What parents and grandparents could not teach the young could be taught by teachers hired by the community and "boarded around" so as to cut their fees. Farmers built the schools. Each family was its own retirement, welfare, and employment agency. There were always chores for the feebleminded, the illiterate, the cripples, the aged, and even the blind. Dependent women with children, who account for 80 per cent of the modern city's welfare cases, were self-sustaining on the family farm. There was no such thing as unemployment. There was always enough to eat.

The overriding fear was of taxation. It alone could undermine the system. Or so it was believed. The appropriate religion was Calvinist—a faith of convenience, for it flattered the agrarian's economics, his self-reliance, and appeased his disdain for the poor, who must have been lazy and sinful not to have acquired land. This environment served the majority in the nineteenth century, but, even then, it never existed for slaves, nor for the minority who lived in cities. But those for whom it did exist were reared in its culture of thrift, hard labor, self-reliance, and distrust for big government as well as big business. Wall Street was as much anathema as Washington. The one manipulated prices; the other spent too much. The attitudes, ideals, and virtues of that culture continue to exert powerful influence over the thinking and social customs of contemporary urban Americans even though the environment which nurtured them has almost vanished.

The Urban Mind—Art Appreciation

An urban mind, appropriate to the national-universal technological systems which now provide our resources, does not exist. We are still a bunch of rural-minded farm refugees trying to function in an urban environment. We have built a new kind of shell but our culture is still agrarian in the way it conditions our minds—in the values, goals, and beliefs which it fosters.

The National Gallery of Art lends costly framed reproductions of its masterpieces to influential government officials. In the last year of the Johnson Administration, it was reported that Wilbur J. Cohen, Secretary of Health, Education, and Welfare, borrowed two Monets. Senator Charles G. Percy had a Cézanne, a Vlaminck, a Whistler, and a Matisse. Senator Everett McKinley Dirksen had two Rembrandts, a Canaletto, a Fragonard, and Dali's "Sacrament of the Last Supper." Statistics on bureaucratic and Congressional taste showed a preference for the conventional, classical, and safe. If the Nixon Administration starts taking out Jackson Pollocks, Mirós, Klees, and Picassos, we are in for a genuine happening rather than a reproduction.

In the Johnsonian years, landscapes held a long lead over still lifes while abstracts were as rare as abstract thinking. As an avid patron of publicly supplied aesthetics, former Secretary of Agriculture Orville L. Freeman chose as a favorite a stylized view of cattle roaming among the dunes of Padre Island, Texas. "It has a sense of scope," commented the Secretary, appreciatively. "I like the struggle between the sand and the vegetation, the movement of cattle far away. It's a good, rugged outdoor picture—pertinent to the kind of thing I'm doing here in Washington." [14]

As official Washington pursues cultural uplift, someday it may discover the "New New Realism." Just as it once comprehended a struggle between sand and vegetation, it may someday comprehend the struggles of the urban mind to rid itself of classical agrarian mythology. When they can grasp the ideas that agitate modern artists bureaucrats and Congress may become contemporary.

The biological prerequisites for life in the city are no different from those for life on the farm. The inhabitant requires food, shelter, and security. Its society must include him. However, there is a world of difference between town and country in the ways the ecologies work. The farm is a natural environment; the city is a synthetic one. Seeds are not planted in the streets to raise food. Trees in the parks are not cut to build shelters. security is the ownership of talent, not land. Acceptance into the organizational network of the city is as essential as membership in the family on a farm. The family is an organic unit; the institutional network is a cultural artifact. All the city's resources are man-made, man-assembled, man-distributed by its networks. Affiliation with the networks is man-arranged.

An abstract ecological diagram of the city looks different from the diagram of the farm with its homestead surrounded by land, surrounded by fences. The city has no physical fences, only organizational barriers. Lands are neither the basis of employment nor the sources of resources. City populations are concentrated, not dispersed. In Diagram 2 the four families of Diagram 1 have left and moved into the city. They live compactly, relying upon organizational place rather than physical space. Survival depends upon cooperation, not upon rugged individualism. Muscular energy is relatively valueless. Electricity is cheaper. Talent brings a premium. Skill is essential. Security is affiliation with the institutional network and its all-risk birth-to-death social insurance and fringe-benefit policies. The interwoven strands in the symbolic sketch of the city represent institutional networks. The individual who is not "in" is "out."

The family no longer is its own educator, employer, welfare and retirement agency. Without its land it cannot give jobs to its illiterate, feebleminded, aged, crippled, blind, and

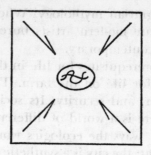

women with dependent children. In the city, an employer must make a profit on the employment of an employee; otherwise he will not employ him. As technology is refined, the cut-off point of profitable employment is raised, and the submarginal are stranded. On the farm, no one was cut off as submarginal. Some were not paid, but no one went hungry. On the farm, food was eaten before surpluses were sold. Hungry families in the city have surpluses of labor and surpluses of time, but they are inedible.

The fallacy of the agrarian ecological system was that there were not enough farms to go around. A farmer without land was like a city man without a job. The city can make a better environment for mass populations because it can create skills and it can create jobs. It can create a society of responsibility to carry out the biological security functions that were a family responsibility on the farm. Agrarian societies could not decently support mass populations because they could not create land. Nature made only so much land that could be developed into farms. The natural environment is a closed system and humanity now exceeds its limits.

The city is an open system. Science and technology steadily increase the environment's capability to employ resources. There is no limit to the growth of intelligence. The synthetic urban environment is anti-entropic. Its usable energy is increasing rather than decreasing. Cities have the generative capabilities to increase the relative effectiveness of resources in proportion to the needs of people. This capability may be expressed by the equation $\frac{R}{P} = f(I)$, which says simply that total resources (R) divided by total population (P) allows a per capita consumption (f) that is a function of intelligence (I). As the cumulative "know-how" of intelligence increases through research and development, living standards rise if talents are upgraded faster than people multiply. The city's job is to cultivate intelligence and organize it into productive systems just as it was the farmer's job to cultivate land. The difference is that human intelligence, which is metaphysical, weightless, and anti-entropic, is an aspect of nature that is capable of limitless growth. Land, on the other hand, is physical. It is limited. Its energy outputs are entropic. Its potential is finite.

As mankind multiplies where the ecology is agrarian, greater demands tax limited land supplies. Stratified societies emerge. Land-possessors line up their armies, priests, and intellectuals so as to keep the landless suppressed, superstitious, and illiterate. This is the way two-thirds of humanity is boxed in today in underdeveloped countries. That situation might be expressed by the equation $\frac{R}{P} = f(FN)$ in which FN is familiar nature. Since nature, as presently familiar to us, has fixed generative capabilities resources per capita shrink as populations increase. People in overpopulated agrarian environments are trapped in a Malthusian dead end. Eventually they will either incite civil wars that could become world wars or the urbanized one-third of humanity will set about systematically to help them urbanize.

Prospects

If the thesis is valid that the modern city is a man-made ecological system, then theoretically its management can be man-determined. To operate effectively it must be managed for change, because the urban ecology is not static. Technologies are improving and populations are increasing. The invention of the technique for invention—the research and development process—has paid off so handsomely that it is now universally respected. It is the creator of the "brain drain." It is responsible for spin-offs of routine cheap-labor jobs from developed to underdeveloped countries. It is responsible for the universal drive to upgrade manpower and productivity. Opportunities to put brains to work now are deliberately built into organizational networks to rationalize their evolution.

As they grow in sophistication the organizational networks become less local, more national and international. Geographic limits are eliminated. The farm fence and local political district lines no longer are meaningful, influential economic boundaries. The urbanite whose roots are in the national institutional network rather than in the local soil is economically liberated. Yet socially and culturally he remains a captive. He is a prisoner of our vestigial agrarian mentalities.

While the private economy is rationalized by the mergers of business and industry into national and international conglomerates there is no comparable rationalization of the public's business. A Brazilian depositor putting money in a Swiss bank helps to finance a Dutch corporation that is part of an international conglomerate with mines in Africa plus a research-development affiliate in the United States which supplies new techniques to a British manufacturer who assembles components from Korea and Hong Kong to put into a machine sent to Canada to turn out products exported to Australia. This is coordination. But while such an efficient international network of private interests and specialties is put together for the more economical production of resources, local governments in the United States still operate as if the world were inhabited by farmers. They try to finance their public services to individuals and to business and industry by levies against property and sales as though land were still the source of wealth. There is nothing in the domain of public enterprise that is in any way comparable to the articulate, sophisticated coordination of inputs and outputs in private enterprise.

Farmers oppose the taxation of land because it is a levy against their security—their source of livelihood. They oppose big government except, of course, when it pays big subsidies to them not to work. Government cannot increase the productivity of land by law or by spending. To make the soil yield is the individual, self-reliant farmer's job. The agrarian wants government to stay out of the social-security and welfare business because the farm has always been its own social-security and welfare agency. The urbanite agrees if his mind is still conditioned by a culturally derived agrarian code of values. But his actual demands for elaborate public services contradict his ideology. Real life interferes with obsolete tenets. Actions conflict with attitudes. It is all part of the cultural confusion generated by a shift of the bulk of the population from the old agrarian to the new urban ecology with its totally different resource base, social organization, and corresponding demands upon the mind to think in new terms.

Prompted by his instincts for survival the modern urbanite insists upon big government services while he cherishes the idea of small government expenditures. He demands an elaborate public education for his children so that they will qualify for affiliation in the economic network. He wants a public social-security system to replace the farm's land-based family-security system. He votes for a costly public transportation network of highways, waterways and airways. He approves of a plush public research-development budget to underwrite technological innovation. Most extravagant of all, he endorses a war machine to keep as much as possible of the underdeveloped world within his international economic network.

These expensive demands upon government for public

services bear no relation to the old-time insistence upon parsimonious government. For good reason. The farmer needed little government service and taxation threatened to confiscate his land. Today security is based upon education and the vigor of the socioeconomic institutional network. Big spending by government is necessary to provide this underpinning. A very large share of the cost of the synthetic environment must be paid for by big expenditures by government. Private persons and private corporations will not seriously engage in enterprises which lose money rather than earn profits.

Since the principal source of wealth in the synthetic urban environment is talent rather than land it is rational that talent should be the principal target of taxation. The income tax levies against the skills and abilities of individuals and corporations. It is a return to government for its investment in the educations of people, its support of industrial research-development, and the public services which support the careers of persons and corporations. What is irrational about the income tax is that it goes chiefly to the Federal Government rather than to the localities and the states, which have the greatest responsibility for constructing and maintaining the public's share of the synthetic environment.

The agrarian's insistence that local and state governments be chiefly responsible for public services now strangles and distorts government's commitment to the synthetic environment. The Federal Government, controlling the principal revenues, those revenues being derived from the taxation of talents, is least obliged to finance the development of talent. Thus it is that local and state governments, which are under the financial constraints of an agrarian culture that levied on lands and sales, must finance the public services of the new urban ecology. The job cannot be done.

It is now up to all levels of government, Federal, state, and local, to develop the same high degree of network coordination that characterizes modern business and industry. Geographic boundary lines have been supplanted in significance by organizational networks that are not tied to place. Modern organizations cross all political boundary lines. Unlike farms they are not fixed in space. Inhabitants no longer derive their ecological prerequisites of food, shelter, and security from a geographic habitat. Institutional place has been substituted for geographic place. Nevertheless, the responsibilities of local, state, and Federal governments, as now defined, relate to the geography of an agrarian culture. They do not correspond to the non-geographic institutional character of the synthetic urban environment.

According to our ecological theory of the city as it has been so far developed food, shelter, and security have become a matter of synthetic resource production. Resources, in turn, result from the generation and exploitation of intelligence, which is capable of infinite expansion under favorable auspices. Such auspices call for the most skillful collaboration of private and public enterprises, for both are engaged in mutually reinforcing activities. Private enterprise has already integrated its operations nationally and, to an accelerating extent, internationally. Long overdue is an equally integrated public service system that can collaborate more articulately with private enterprise, respond adequately to the physiological and psychological needs of individuals, and guide the development of a physical shell that is both beautiful and functional.

4

Governments and Budgets

There are 70,726 units of local government in the United States which have the power to tax. These mini-governments range from obscure suburban school districts to the City of New York. Collectively they are responsible for most of the public services that directly affect the quality of our daily lives. They support our schools, pave our streets, give fire and police protection, provide most public recreation facilities, and take care of water, sewage, and garbage services. Yet they collect less than one-fifth of all public revenues.[1]

The Federal Government grabs off two-thirds of all tax monies collected from the American people, but it is responsible for only a minute fraction of the public services that make our synthetic environment livable. Over half of all federal revenues go to support the military establishment. Currently Washington is spending about two and a half times as much on military gear and personnel as is collected in taxes by all units of local government. In 1967, the Pentagon spent $70.1 billion while the 70,726 units of local government collected $29.3 billion in taxes. Most of the remainder of the federal wealth has been used to pay interest on the national debt, finance veterans' benefits, support foreign policy, and subsidize agriculture.[2]

Washington's outlays for welfare have ranged from a low of 3.1 per cent of its total non-trust funded expenditures in 1965 to a high of 4.6 per cent in 1969.[3] Welfare or public assistance costs account for an average of 7 per cent of local and state budgets. New York City in fiscal year 1969-70 will spend 23 per cent of its budget on public assistance. It catches a disproportionately large share of the national overflow of impoverished rural refugees from Puerto Rico, the South, and Appalachia. The fifty states are responsible particularly for higher education, mental hospitals, and state highways. Like localities they, too, collect less than one-fifth of all the public wealth derived strictly from taxes. In 1967, while the 70,726 localities collected the $29.3 billion in taxes already mentioned, the states collected $31.9 billion; the Federal Government collected $115.1 billion.[4] As we shall note later, governments have other sources of revenue besides taxes. For instance, the Federal Government takes in several billion dollars more in Social Security premiums than it pays out. It uses this surplus Social Security income to defray other government expenses, rather than to divide it among the aged and disabled for whom it is collected. Some localities operate utilities for profit and some states operate liquor stores.

No other national government of a great world power piles so much responsibility for public services onto the backs of financially weak and financially unequal local units of government. Compilations of international statistics on the total collection of taxes by all levels of government show that most industrial nations collect a higher percentage of gross national product in taxes and Social Security premiums than the United States. Only Russia and China spend as much on military affairs. The consequence is a higher rate of government spending on public services in other urbanized but less militaristic countries. A study by the Organization for Economic Cooperation and Development in Paris shows that in France, all tax collections amount to 38.5 per cent of GNP as compared with 27.3 per cent in the United States. In West Germany, taxes amount to 34.4 per cent of GNP; in Italy, 29.6 per cent; in the United Kingdom, 28.6 per cent. As for military spending, statistics compiled by Robert McConnell of Vancouver's *Province* show that the United States leads the pack with 7.9 per cent of GNP. France spends 4.8 per cent, Sweden 4.6 per cent, the United Kingdom 6.1 per cent, Norway 4.3 per cent, and Canada 2.2 per cent. Another study by the U. S. Arms Control and Disarmament Agency reports that in 1965 while the United States spent 7.6 per cent of its GNP on military goods and services, Russia spent between 7 and 8 per cent and China spent 7.9 per cent. Apparently those nations most strongly committed to the use of force to impose their ideologies have less to spend to put those ideologies into practice at home.

In Canada, the provinces share with localities the support of elementary and secondary education, which is the costliest of all local public responsibilities in the United States. In European countries and Japan, national governments pick up most of the tab for public instruction. In the United States, the support of education accounts for about 48 per cent of all local government outlays and 27 per cent of all public expenditures by states. For the fiscal year 1967, the Federal Government of the United States contributed $2.3 billion out of a total bill of $40.5 billion for public primary, secondary, and higher education. Localities paid 71.1 per cent of the total, states 23.2 per cent. Washington's share was 5.7 per cent.[5]

The U. S. Conference of Mayors predicted in 1968 that within the following decade, American cities would spend $738 billion and that less than 10 per cent of these funds would come as grants-in-aid from the federal treasury unless present priorities were revised. The crisis condition of the

American city is directly related to the fact that the weakest, most highly fractionated level of government is responsible for most of the public services and facilities that go into the makeup of our synthetic environment.

While the private economy is dominated by the strongest, smartest, best-financed, and articulately interrelated national corporations, the public economy at the local level, where it affects the quality of our lives, is poorly financed and managed by weaklings. There is nothing in the coordination of government operations between local, state, and national levels that is comparable to the overlapping memberships in the boards of directors of great private corporations. The boards of directors of America's top 100 corporations are a sensitive, knowledgeable network of keen minds with dovetailing interests and awarenesses. In 1966 they captained the sales of $211.7 billion in goods and services. This was almost as much as the $225.6 billion in goods and services produced by all levels of government that same year.[6] Not until its closing days did the 90th Congress pass the "Intergovernmental Cooperation Act of 1968" which spelled out the preliminary guidelines for orderly communication on matters of mutual interest between federal agencies, the governors of states, and local authorities.

In the spring of 1969, it was too early to predict what the Nixon Administration would do but it was evident that the new president had under review both problems and budgets. In April the first Nixon changes in the Johnson budget for 1970 were announced. They were not dramatic but they showed some promise. It was proposed that $322 million in rising costs of aid to dependent children should be absorbed by the Federal Government rather than by states and localities. Such an increase, the Nixon Administration declared, would impose "a nearly intolerable burden on states and local jurisdictions." There was talk, too, of a greatly expanded federal subsidy of food stamp aid to the hungry, but the details were not spelled out. At the same time, small cuts were recommended in the "pork barrel" appropriations for reclamation and power projects by the Department of the Interior and the rivers and harbors schemes of the Army Engineers.

Such changes in priorities were long overdue, and they needed to be expressed in far more emphatic terms in future budgets. The first real Nixon budget for fiscal 1971 would tell whether or not Washington was prepared to deal with the public problems that confront America at state and local levels or continue in the Johnsonian rut. Obviously, the war in Vietnam would have to end so that the Pentagon's swollen defense budget, which reached $80.5 billion in 1968, could be cut back to $50.9 billion, where it had been in 1964 before escalation under Johnson. The $30 billion saved would be needed for any serious attention to the domestic needs of a polarizing urban society.

The powerful Federal Government, which is privileged to tap the richest sources of public revenue through personal and corporate income taxes, assumes at present only token responsibility for the public share of the man-made urban habitat. Furthermore, in the past it has been philosophically disposed to reject such responsibility. During his last year in office, President Lyndon Johnson repeatedly emphasized that the financial responsibility for supporting America's cities "belongs to local government and the private sector." The private sector takes care very well of providing all goods and services that yield a profit, but since most public services at the local level are unprofitable, this means that the weakest governments have the severest environmental responsibilities.

Local governments were not always so poor. Even in the depression year of 1932, they were relatively better off than they are today. At that time, they collected fifty cents of every tax dollar, and the states collected twenty cents, while the Federal Government collected thirty cents. Now localities collect less than seventeen cents of every dollar extracted from the taxpayer, and the states collect eighteen cents, while the Federal Government collects over sixty-five cents.[7] This reversal in who gets what share of the total tax take is of supreme significance when it comes to explaining why the quality of local public services is worse today than during the Depression despite current economic prosperity.

While localities remain just as responsible for public services as they were in 1932, their share of the public tax dollar is now only one-third of what it was before World War II. At that time, the Federal Government took over as the big collector of taxes but assumed only minor responsibilities for those public services that make the environment habitable. It is the total tax bite out of his net earnings which most affects the taxpayer's purse. It is the return in public services which most affects his attitude as to whether or not he gets his money's worth. Therefore, more important than the amount of dollars which each level of government collects is the *proportion* of all tax dollars which each takes in and what each does with its revenues. Today at the local level, where public services mean most in terms of satisfactions, the taxpayer gets only one-third as much for his money as he got in 1932. No wonder he is angry, frustrated, and on the verge of a tax rebellion.

Americans pay ample sums in total taxes. Public services simply are not commensurate with those taxes. The obvious reason is that the purse is weak where the needs are great while a willingness to respond to those needs is weak where the purse is strong. Also, there is no such coordination among the thousands of units of government as there is among the managements of the 100 largest private corporations. It would be hard to imagine a single individual serving simultaneously as a member of the Congress of the United States, a state legislature, and a city council. Yet it is not at all extraordinary for a single person to serve simultaneously as a director of a half-dozen major private corporations. Some men do that and hold public office as well. So it is that the most crucial decisions by private enterprise are coordinated while those that have chiefly to do with the public environment are not. The agrarian conviction that local government should have the greatest public responsibility in order that local voters may restrain public spending has hobbled the cities, but it has not in any way curtailed Washington's ability to tax and spend as it sees fit. It has only relieved Washington of a sense of responsibility for a deepening domestic crisis.

Commission

In 1966, former President Lyndon Johnson created the National Commission on Urban Problems. To head it he named former Senator Paul H. Douglas of Illinois. The Commission submitted its report two years later. It had discovered nothing new. It had not been expected to. To begin with, the appointment of the Commission was an administrative maneuver to put off genuine federal action on issues already fully researched. All the Commission's prime solutions had been proposed long before it published its findings. But those solutions called for changes in the priorities of public spending which the Johnson Administration was not prepared to accept. It was deep in Vietnam. That is where, without having appointed a commission to make a two-year fact-finding feasibility study, it had decided to commit itself and a disproportionate share of the public wealth. The Douglas Commission discovered to no one's amazement that matters like education and public assistance, which commonly are represented as unique local headaches, are, as *The New York Times* put it, "recurrent problems across the nation."

Just after the Douglas Commission made its report, Republican Mayor John Lindsay of New York addressed the Ripon Society's liberal Republican membership. He proposed some guidelines for the incoming Nixon Administration of their own party. National priorities should be revised, he said, "to help secure us from the dangers of domestic collapse." New foreign "traps" such as Thailand should be avoided, said the Mayor, who often had spoken out for the distressed cities and had criticized Vietnam's "endless, debilitating war." Urban finances everywhere were in chaotic condition. The U. S. Conference of Mayors reported that "Among the ten largest cities, nine lost population between 1950 and 1960, most of them white and middle income. The latter all experienced a steady increase, however, in Negro population."

Translated into budgets, the out-migration of the white middle class and the in-migration of destitute Negroes meant increased financial strains for the cities and forced a decrease in the quality of their public services. "Local governments' share of the tax dollar has decreased substantially," the Mayors' report continued, "from 50 cents of each tax dollar in 1930 to about 15 cents today—local governments have been forced to serve a greater number of people having more intensive needs with fewer sources to call upon for increased revenues." [8]

The day after his speech to the Ripon Society, Mayor Lindsay went to Washington to see Wilbur J. Cohen, the outgoing administration's Secretary of Health, Education, and Welfare. Cohen had about one month left to serve before Richard Nixon was to put Robert Finch on the job. Said the Mayor at his meeting with the Secretary, "I have supported for a long time federalization of the entire burden of welfare. No local community can really stand the pressures we're all under." Lindsay's figures showed that the welfare rolls in New York City were rising at the rate of 20,000 per month and that one out of eight persons in his city was on relief. Cohen agreed with the Mayor. He, too, had researched the matter and had already recommended that the Federal Government should take over the welfare program and run it according to uniform national standards. Cities which displayed some humanity were catching the rejects of other communities that were starving them out.⁹ The hitch, of course, was that Secretary Cohen's boss and the Congress did not agree with him. Humanism was not popular in Washington, yet the roots of poverty were not local; they were national.

Placed upon the desk of the incoming Nixon Administration, the report of Senator Douglas' National Commission on Urban Problems, with all of its neatly summarized analyses, was unlikely to change Washington's official viewpoint. When questioned about his own attitude toward the Federal Government's responsibility to lift welfare burdens from the backs of cities, Cohen's successor, Robert Finch, hedged. He could not agree that the time is now. However, he said he was convinced "that down the road we will probably have to assume a greater share of the burden. The question is how."

The answer, as everyone knows, is with money. Just a small amount of the monies going to the military for overkill and to agriculture for overproduction would do it. Then why not make the switch? Possibly the proper thing to do would be to appoint a new National Commission on Urban Problems and ask it to report back in four years.

Certainly the time was not ripe for any dramatic change of course. For one thing, the big cities that were in the worst trouble with the largest Negro populations did not go to President Nixon in the election. "It is perfectly clear that we hardly owe our election to the Negro community," remarked Secretary Finch when interviewed on the matter of welfare in the ghetto cities. "In a way, we get a kind of freedom out of this in terms of options because we can deal directly with this problem without any hint of political obligation." Since the name of the game was "political obligation" Stokely Carmichael could not have stated the case for black power more adroitly.

After the election of Richard Nixon to the Presidency, New York's Republican Governor Nelson Rockefeller recommended the federalization of all welfare programs before a conference of governors. He pointed out that New York pays recipients of aid to dependent children $50.83 a month while Mississippi pays $7.90. As a consequence desperate Negro mothers in Mississippi and other Deep South states move to New York when they are displaced from farm jobs by mechanization. Governor Ronald Reagan of California took exception to Rockefeller's suggestions. The solution, he said, is to halt the migrations of destitute persons from poorer states to richer ones by tightening residency requirements. On April 21, 1969, the U. S. Supreme Court ruled that the imposition by states of residency requirements upon applicants for welfare is unconstitutional. However, states still differ in their welfare standards. Congressman Roman C. Pucinski of Illinois says that in his state, 49 per cent of the persons on welfare come from Mississippi where welfare standards are maintained at a subhuman level to force poor people to migrate.[10]

While federal welfare payments have been made for over thirty years to land-owning farmers without any requirement for matching funds from states or localities, all federal aids to indigent welfare recipients must be supplemented with matching appropriations by states and localities. There is, therefore, no effective local opposition to million-dollar federal give-aways to prosperous farmers but there is passionate objection to even slight increases in the welfare budgets of poverty-stricken families driven off the farms. Washington could assume almost the full cost of the nation's public assistance program as now funded without any increase in its budget if it ceased to pay subsidies to its most successful farmers and to buy their surplus commodities. The problem is not money but attitude. Former director of the Bureau of the Budget Kermit Gordon has said, "About 80 per cent of our farm assistance goes to one million farmers whose average income exceeds $9,500. The other 20 per cent of assistance is spread thinly among the remaining 2,500,000 farmers." [11] Farm subsidy programs have become particularly discriminatory now that the Department of Agriculture declares its programs are aimed at achieving parity income for "adequate size commercial farms, but not necessarily for small farms." *Adequate* means grossing more than $10,000 a year in sales. A Department of Agriculture Under Secretary has indicated that farms smaller than this would have to look first to departments other than his for assistance.

Budgets and Policy

Whatever the rhetoric of politics, the real statements of public policy are the budgets of governments. An effective appraisal of any government's responses to the needs of people is impossible without an overview of current spending patterns. Suggestions for change make sense only in that wider context. Without a grasp of the overall budget pattern, the masses of data simply add up to confusion. "The executive branch of the Federal Government," observes *The New York Times,* "has in the Bureau of the Budget perhaps the nearest approach to an organization for rational consideration of priorities, and its conclusions are embodied in the President's budget message annually." The Congress has nothing equivalent to the President's statement of priorities. Thus it reacts piecemeal to executive suggestion but formulates no coherent anticipatory policy of its own. Not one out of 100 Senators or one out of 435 Representatives ever makes a full quantitative declaration of how he would propose to allocate the federal wealth. "Various appropriation bills tend to be considered in isolation from each other, and decisions on quite important individual items often reflect the predilections or prejudices of particularly influential individuals or small groups. What is needed," suggests the *Times,* "is an overhaul of the manner in which Congress makes decisions . . . to make sure that we are weighing competing demands of alternative needs." [12] Possibly just keeping a running scoreboard of appropriations in the House and Senate chambers would give legislators and the public a quantitative measure of their senses of priorities.

The only way to tell whether or not a government has acquired a working concept of the urban age and its social responsibilities is to examine how it spends the public purse. In those terms, the Federal Government of the United States is a warfare, not a welfare, state. In 1968, Washington spent $134.3 billion in taxes to conduct its affairs. This sum excludes self-sustaining trust fund expenditures which were estimated by the Bureau of the Budget at $44.7 billion. The sum of $85.2 billion was spent on the military, including outlays for atomic energy and space exploration. Veterans' benefits came to an additional $6.9 billion. Interest on the national debt, nearly all of which resulted from previous military spending, raised the total by another $13.7 billion. Thus outlays for present, past, and future warfare came to $105.8 billion or 78 per cent of all federal spending in 1968. In 1968 the Vietnam war alone cost an estimated $30 billion —a sum exceeding the $29.3 billion which was the total of all taxes collected by all 70,726 units of local government in 1967.[13] These allocations of the public wealth constitute the clearest, simplest statement of the priorities that shape American public policy. So it was that in 1968 Washington had only $29.1 billion or 21.5 per cent of all its non-trust-funded appropriations left to attend to other responsibilities such as international affairs, agriculture, and general services, including aid to states and cities for social welfare, housing, transportation, etc.

Trustee

Apart from its tax-supported functions, Washington serves as administrator and trustee for a number of compulsory insurance and trust fund accounts such as the Old Age and Survivors Insurance Trust Fund (Social Security), the Federal Disability Insurance Trust Fund, Health Insurance Trust funds, Unemployment Trust Fund, Railroad Retirement accounts, Federal Employees Retirement funds, the Highway Trust Fund, and Veterans Life Insurance funds. All the disbursements made under these funds are paid for by their beneficiaries or are earned as the fringe benefits of employment. They are not supported by general taxation. They should not, therefore, be lumped together with regular public expenses.

The government's trust and insurance funds could just as well be managed by private corporations. In fact participants would probably be better compensated if trust funds were managed by private industry since the Federal Government helps itself to trust fund surpluses whenever it is short of cash and it does not bother to repay them. In private business this would be called embezzlement. No person enjoys the benefits of these funds who does not contribute to them. Social Security, for instance, is not available to the poorest, least secure of all citizens because they are not covered by the legislation and do not make contributions. Others who do contribute receive benefits according to what they have contributed, not according to what they might need. In 1967 federal insurance trust funds disbursed $38.5 billion in benefits, but they took in $44.7 billion in premiums. By these commercial dealings, Washington came out ahead with a surplus of $6.2 billion. It was an outright violation of C. Northcote Parkinson's 3rd Law that "all nationalized industries tend to go bankrupt." Obviously the trust funds are not an average "nationalized industry." Like the Post Office, the management of trust funds should be handed over to private industry as a public utility—privately managed but publicly regulated.

It is necessary to clarify the distinction between the general public expenses of government and the disbursements of insurance and trust funds because in the recent publicity about public finance, they have been lumped together. This confuses nearly everyone. Former President Lyndon Johnson introduced the practice. He called it the "unified budget" concept. Lumping the two made Washington look as if it believed in helping the poor when in fact trust fund surpluses were diverted to cover normal government expenditures which should have been paid for by direct taxation.

In the discussion of government budgets which follows, trust fund incomes and disbursements are omitted unless specifically referred to. Also omitted are the incomes and expenditures of liquor stores and utility companies operated by state and local governments. These, too, are commercial profit-making enterprises, not tax-supported public services. They are socialist business activities inconsistent with our free enterprise philosophy. Although Washington's "unified budget" concept now is operational, it still is possible to separate insurance and trust fund accounts by a detailed examination of *The Budget of the United States Government.* This annual publication runs to 551 pages in its 1970 edition.

When political orators talk about astronomical budgets for social welfare, they refer to the new "unified budget" with its accounts padded with self-supporting and profit-making trust fund operations. For instance, in fiscal year 1964, the last John F. Kennedy budget, the Department of Health, Education, and Welfare spent $5.5 billion. In fiscal 1968, the last Johnson year, the same department spent $40.6 billion— an eightfold jump. The catch, of course, is that in 1964 self-supporting trust fund expenditures were not included. In 1968 trust fund disbursements alone accounted for $29.2 billion of HEW's outlays. Thus the real increase in HEW's "Great Society" programs was $5.9 billion, not $35.1 billion.

In addition to HEW's non-trust fund social service programs costing $11.4 billion, the office of the President allocated another $1.9 billion to the Office of Economic Opportunity to finance community development programs, Head Start, and manpower training. Thus it could be said that the Johnson Administration in 1968 spent a total of $13.3 billion on HEW and OEO social welfare programs compared with the Kennedy outlay of $5.5 billion in 1964. But that would be misleading because under President Kennedy the Federal Administrative Budget was separated from the Federal Trust Fund Budget.

By combining the two budgets into a "unified budget" the Johnson Administration was able to transfer excess Social Security and other trust fund investments by millions of Americans to the payment of other government expenses without obviously drawing attention to the fact. In 1968, Federal social insurance trust fund premium payments, principally for Social Security, amounted to $34.6 billion while disbursements under these trust funds were only $29.2 billion. Instead of paying beneficiaries of these trust funds the full incomes from them, the Federal Government diverted $5.4 billion to general administrative activities. The Johnson Administration in 1968 spent $7.8 billion more on HEW and OEO than the Kennedy Administration but it could be said that $5.4 billion of that amount came from shortchanging the intended beneficiaries of the trust funds.

The Nixon Administration apparently intends to continue with the "unified budget" despite the obvious temptation it offers to divert trust fund surpluses to the payment of ordinary administrative expenses. However, it may dip less into Social Security funds. The last Johnson budget, submitted in January, 1969, called for an increase in Social Security payments. It proposed to raise the present 9.6 per cent contribution rate (4.8 per cent from employee and 4.8 per cent from employer) to 10.4 per cent—5.2 per cent from employee and 5.2 per cent from employer—effective January 1, 1970. In addition, President Johnson recommended that beginning July 1, 1969, the taxable wage should be $9,000 per year rather than $7,800. Together these increases in Social Security premiums were expected to finance a 10 per cent increase in Social Security payments to the elderly and handicapped now receiving monthly checks. This increase was estimated at $1.6 billion. Under the Johnson budget for fiscal 1970, total social insurance trust fund receipts were estimated at $45.9 billion while outlays were estimated at $42.9 billion—returning a net profit to Washington of $3.0 billion.

In his April revisions of the Johnson budget, President Nixon did not propose to change the scheduled increase in payroll deductions for Social Security. He did, however, suggest that the planned increase in benefits should be cut from 10 to 7 per cent and that these increases should be delayed until checks were written for mailing March, 1970. In this way the original estimated benefit increase of $1.6 billion would have been cut back to an estimated $0.6 billion—adding a one-billion-dollar profit to the $3.0 billion anticipated.

These details were spelled out in the 1970 edition of *The Budget of the United States Government* and in the *Congressional Record* of April 16, 1969. Reaction in Congress was sharp. "Simply stated, the Nixon proposal," said Representative Phillip Burton of California, "adds a 'surplus' to the trust fund of $1 billion by taking it out of the 'hides' of the poorest people in the country. Nixon is suggesting that the 25.5 million Social Security beneficiaries, about 75 per cent of whom are aged, will in effect be 'soaked' to the tune of $1 billion of reduced benefits." On September 25, President Nixon responded to the criticism. He proposed that the full 10 per cent increase in benefits be restored, beginning with checks to be mailed on April 1, 1970. The President also proposed a new payroll deduction schedule. Employee and employer contributions would rise to 5.1 per cent in 1971, not 1970. The wage base would rise to $9,000 on January 1, 1972, not July 1, 1969, as recommended by President Johnson.

HEW

Who is helped by HEW, which generally is pictured as a welfare agency for the poor? If HEW's 1968 regular tax supported budget of $11.4 billion is examined in detail, it is discovered that most of what it spends goes to serve the middle-class majority. For instance, the Office of Education disbursed $3.5 billion. Of this amount, $1.8 billion went chiefly to subsidize general elementary, secondary, and vocational education. Some was spent for research and planning programs rather than for schools. Another $506 million was granted to improve facilities and instruction in school districts where large numbers of federal employees are resident, chiefly nice suburban schools around military installations. An additional $144 million went for defense education grants chiefly at the college level. Another $879 million went to institutions of higher education for buildings, equipment, research, and fellowships. Educational improvement for the handicapped was supported with $41 million.

Genuine welfare programs for the poor and underprivileged, as administered by the Social and Rehabilitation Service of HEW, amounted to $5.9 billion. Of these funds, $5.3 billion were grants to states for such public assistance programs as aid to families with dependent children and Medicaid. In the last Kennedy Administration budget of fiscal year 1964, the grants to states for public assistance were $2.78 billion. As far as the genuine poor were concerned, the "Great Society" HEW budget of 1968 added $2.5 billion to their relief. Meanwhile the budget of the Department of Defense programs rose from $50.9 billion under Kennedy in 1964 to $80.5 billion under Johnson in 1968—an increase of $29.6 billion. The estimated budget for 1969 showed the disparity continuing—while the Department of Defense budget was estimated at $79.6 billion, grants to states for public assistance were estimated at $6.3 billion. The 1969 budget for the Department of Agriculture was estimated at $8.4 billion, of which only $0.65 billion was spent on food stamps and surplus commodities for the American poor, including school lunch programs for needy children.

A few years ago when the mayors of American cities asked

Congress to create a Department of Urban Affairs, the influential *Farm Journal* editorialized against it for fear that it would become a channel for the flow of federal wealth to help City Hall with its growing problems. "Even the President has argued that since we have a Department of Agriculture, a department for the more numerous city people is needed," proclaimed editor Wheeler McMillen. "How would a DUA benefit the whole nation as the USDA has done? . . . Two things it certainly would do. It would encourage not only the big cities, but the small ones to take their tin cups to Washington whenever they need a few firewagons or street sweeper's brooms. The sense of local responsibility would be destroyed. And, number two, it would become a magnificent way to spend more money. Cities that do not pay their own bills endanger self-government's future." [14] Evidently there was little fear among the farm readership that their own rugged individualism would be undermined by having their bills paid for them by the urban taxpayer. In 1968 all taxes paid by farmers to all levels of government amounted to $1.7 billion. However, federal subsidies to farmers just for price support and related programs were estimated by the Bureau of the Budget to have been $5.79 billion for the year July 1968-June 1969. In the same year the Department of Housing and Urban Development (which had been established despite agrarian objection) spent $2.0 billion in federal funds.

The Tax Base

Localities and states are financially unable to carry the burden of public services for an urban age in which all communities are part of a national system of cities with populations shifting constantly from one to another. It is estimated that one American family in five moves every year. Modern cities exist on a tax base inherited from a nineteenth-century agrarian society in which people were tied to the same piece of land for generations. Localities, even now, derive 87 per cent of their tax collections from levies against properties. States obtain three-fifths of their tax collections from levies against sales. Yet it is clear that most incomes in an urban society are not derived from working land or from buying and selling in an old-fashioned market place. The great majority of people, as Herman Miller has explained, get their wages and salaries by selling their skills and talents to an employer. This goes for most clerks and managers of retail establishments. The income tax is the only one that taxes talents and skills, the primary base of modern productivity. The income tax rises automatically with gross national product and the Federal Government takes almost all of it. States get a little. Localities for the most part get none. A few get driblets.

Comparative Wealth

Even when trust funds, state liquor sales, and local utility sales are omitted (as they are in the totals given below), governments have other sources of revenues besides taxes. They come under the general heading of "user charges." User charges differ from taxes in that only "users" pay charges. For instance, in 1967 the Federal Government collected $15.7 billion in this manner, chiefly for postal services, sales and leases of natural resources, and interest on money loaned. States collected $5.8 billion, chiefly as school tuitions and interest charges. Localities collected $9.0 billion, chiefly through school tuitions, school lunch sales, hospital fees, interest, and general charges.[15]

Out of the total $206.8 billion collected by all levels of government strictly as taxes and user charges (excluding trust fund and business incomes), the Federal establishment took in 63.3 per cent, states 18.2 per cent, and localities 18.5 per cent. The really big revenues were $95.5 billion in personal and corporate income taxes paid to the Federal Government, $18.6 billion in sales and excise taxes collected by states, and $25.4 billion in property taxes collected by localities. *Personal* income taxes paid to Washington totaled $61.5 billion. That amount considerably exceeded the $48.0 billion collected by all states and localities through sales and property taxes. However, that sum of $61.5 billion collected by the Federal Government from every individual income-tax payer in the country fell far short of the Pentagon's bill of $70.1 billion for the same year, 1967.[16]

Until Washington becomes as responsive to the domestic needs of its citizens and their public environment as it is now to international power politics and its own military bureaucracy, there is little hope for any impressive improvement either in social services or in the public facilities of cities. At the moment, it is only the Federal Government which has enough tax income to truly serve the public need. Only federal revenues, derived from the source that increases automatically with gross national product and technological evolution, can respond to the requirements of the synthetic environment that generates the growing gross national product.

Localities, sustained by the property tax, drop further behind. Local tax revenues do not rise automatically with inflation or with gross national product. The Advisory Commission on Intergovernmental Relations estimates that less than half of the increase in state tax collections over the past fifteen years was generated by old taxes in response to national growth. It reports that the major part of the increase came from new and increased taxes. Charles J. Swick, a former director of the Bureau of the Budget, calls this living on the brink of financial insecurity "a kind of political parlor game akin to Russian roulette at election time." People can get fed up at local and state levels and blow the whistle.

When 500,000 Californians signed a petition to limit local property taxes to 1 per cent of property market values and restrict the use of such revenues to "property-related" public services such as street construction and sewage facilities, there was panic in Sacramento. The logic of property taxes for services to property did not appeal to the State House. It was recognized that the responsibility for "people-related" services, to the tune of $2.5 billion, would thereby be shifted from localities to the state. Since the state was far from being on a revenue base of a people tax for people services, the shift could have meant a hike in California's state sales tax from 5 per cent to 12 per cent. "It is the most dangerous, deceptive measure to be presented to the voters of California in recent times," remarked the state's Director of Finance, Caspar Weinberger. "It would effectively destroy local government and could seriously injure the state's credit."

To this argument Los Angeles County's tax assessor, Philip E. Watson, retorted, "Nonsense. The property tax is the most vicious and confiscatory tax we have. . . . It is the responsibility of the legislature to work out a fair and equitable, broadly based tax structure to provide the necessary substitute revenues for school and welfare costs. . . ." [17] If localities with their limited tax bases were to shift their "people-related" obligations to states and the states in turn were to shift them to Washington, they would only be doing what is the practice in most of the world's progressive industrial nations. It would in effect shift these modern responsibilities of an urban society from the obsolete agrarian tax on property as the mythical source of wealth to talent which is the real source of wealth in all synthetic environments and which is developed by the educational system. Welfare costs simply represent the failure of the educational system to train all able-bodied persons, or of the social insurance system to provide full and complete coverage for all casualties. The 500,000 Californian property holders had raised a vital issue.

Representative Robert W. Kastenmeier recently reported to Congress on the findings of economist Arnold Cantor that state and local government debt grew from less than $50 billion to over $100 billion in the ten years 1956-66 despite the fact that they had doubled their tax levies. "In contrast," the report stated, "over the same period the Federal Government has been able to reduce tax rates and underwrite sharp increases in defense spending while revenues still increased by some 75% and the debt grew by less than 20%." "Western European countries," the report continued, "spend 2-3 times the proportion of their national income on public welfare (broadly defined) than the U. S." [18] So we are back again to the question of priorities, and who is responsible for what.

The economic growth that automatically increases Washington's income puts localities in a constantly worsening position. When gross national product increases and when populations increase and new jobs are created, income taxes produce more revenue. As far as localities are concerned, economic growth and population growth raise the demands for more services and facilities. But tax revenues from the property tax do not go up automatically. As Washington gets richer, localities become relatively poorer. Philip E. Kettell, member of Rhode Island's North Kingstown Town Council, has calculated that if 30,000 families were to move into his community and if each were to live in a new $20,000 house, the tax revenues would bring in $18.6 million annually while the public costs of servicing the new population would be $26 million if each family had two children in school. Economic prosperity would create fiscal depression for local government. This phenomenon is almost universal and explains why after twenty years of almost unbroken prosperity, the American city faces the worst crisis in its history. Economist Wilbur Thompson says, "To grow is to get bigger." As far as localities are concerned that is the heart of their problem. As they prosper economically, they grow in population and expand physically. Their service responsibilities grow at a faster rate than their tax base. The result is an increasing bonded indebtedness; a growing clamor for state and federal aid. All new construction of public facilities costs more than comparable facilities built years ago. The same amount of school space or volume of sewer pipe which served a smaller population and a smaller economy a decade ago costs more per capita to build now than then. Thus if an urban population doubles, local taxes must more than double just to keep up the old level of services. If, in addition, the wealthier citizens move to suburbia, leaving central city stuck with rural refugees and functional illiterates who double-up in the old houses, then the situation becomes downright unmanageable.

The irony of this process is that economic growth directly increases federal income tax revenues. That is what it is supposed to do. It is called the "new economics." Washington runs a deficit which gasses the economy and produces some inflation. With its revenues tied to the income tax, which rises with gross national product and inflation, Washington finds itself automatically richer. At present these automatic raises amount to about $6 billion annually. However, states and localities must build the schools, colleges, streets, roads, and water-sewer systems, and pay the police and fire departments that economic growth and population multiplication demand. They are penalized by prosperity. Their bonded indebtedness increases by $5 billion annually.

It is smart of the Federal Government, both the Congress and the Presidency, to eulogize the agrarian principle of local responsibility for local services while it pockets the profits that result from the economic growth of cities. By accepting the fiscal responsibilities of servicing the growth of populations and physical plant, states and localities do in fact subsidize the Federal Government which grabs the profits of economic growth.

City Pay and Country Living

Because capital and talent are mobile while property is not, it is possible for the middle class to live in suburbia, commute to central city to work and collect wages for their talents while making little, if any, contribution to the city's maintenance expenses. The Federal Government taxes their incomes; the suburbs tax their properties; the states collect their sales taxes. The city goes into debt for being at their convenience. Yet "Business generally requires more public services than do residents," reports Richard W. Epps of the Philadelphia Federal Reserve Bank. "A 1 per cent increase in business concentration, measured by the proportion of assessed real estate in business use, leads to between a $2 and a $5 increase in per capita expenditure." [19] No city unless it shifts its primary tax base from property to income can catch the middle class that draws city pay to live a country life. Philadelphia's suburbs spend an average of $103 per capita on the education of their children. Philadelphia city spends $62.

The urban ghetto, which suburbanites like to think is a city problem, was not generated by the city. Most of the misfit people there who account for its social overhead are refugees either from the technological revolution in agriculture or from our segregationist society, which has given them a fifth-rate education and refused to employ them because of their color. In part they are the Federal Government's gift to the city—the consequence of subsidies that encourage the replacement of men with machines. It is ironical that the subsidies that have stimulated the growth of the ghetto were paid out of income taxes earned in the cities while the city must support the human casualties with property tax revenues more appropriate for a rural society.

The suburban community of Scarsdale in Westchester County has one of the finest public school systems in the United States. Scarsdale's wealth is generated in New York City. Of all high school graduates in Scarsdale, 99 per cent go on to college. In East Harlem, New York City, less than 2 per cent of the high school graduates even qualify for college entrance. When Negroes in the Ocean Hill-Brownsville ghetto neighborhood got control of their own school district on an experimental basis, they fired a group of white teachers for incompetence and racist attitudes. This precipitated a city-wide strike of union teachers charging discrimination although the school board had retained other white teachers who made up 70 per cent of their staff. Fifty-two per cent of all New York City schoolchildren are black, and their elementary schools are so bad that not more than 5 per cent of them even get into the city's academic high schools that prepare students for college.

The U. S. Office of Education reports that "A century ago 2 per cent of young Americans entered college. Now, the figure is 50 per cent and still rising. In a Gallup poll, 97 per cent of all parents questioned said they wanted their children to enter college." Scarsdale has achieved the future. New York City's East Harlem is a century behind time. It is not that the city's tax base fails to increase, it is that the city itself, which generates taxes for the Federal Government, is on the wrong tax base. It cannot catch the people who want good public schools. They leave each night on the commuter trains and over the federal interstate highways. "The local tax burden in the central cities, measured against income, is more than 50 per cent greater than in suburbs . . . ," declares Maryland's Senator Joseph Tydings. Furthermore, "The overall expenditure pattern of large central cities indicates an expansion of the 'noneducational' municipal services sector and a fall in the educational outlays for the same cities . . ." [20] More police are hired instead of good teachers. They can be employed for less.

New York, or "Fun City" as it is ironically called, is in the midst of a real estate boom and has been for the past twenty years. Instead of petering out, the boom is accelerating. Summarizing the year 1968, Mayor Lindsay announced that there "has been five times as much office building construction as three years ago . . . What other city has more booming construction?" If the property tax were appropriate for an urban society, New York would be the best place in the world to live. Instead, in the past decade a million whites moved out and a million Negroes and Puerto Ricans moved in. The city collects only one-quarter of 1 per cent payroll tax from its commuters. This adds up to about $200 million. The city's fiscal 1970 expense budget is $6.6 billion.

The white élite who dominate the city's private financial and business interests are in large measure suburbanites. According to labor boss Harry Van Arsdale, president of the Central Labor Council, "Nobody cares about New York City anymore. They all want to get out of it. You go to a meeting of a hundred of the biggest names in New York and the first thing you find out is that at least sixty of them live outside the city. It's the same thing with policemen and firemen and everybody else. Some of them are driving fifty miles each day to get to work and fifty miles more to get home." [21]

City Hall's public payroll accounted for 58 per cent of the 1969 expense budget. Black New York gets very few of the jobs in its own city while whites come in from the suburbs to run the place. *New York Times* editor A. H. Raskin puts it bluntly, "The Irish got there first in police, fire and transit, the Italians in sanitation, the Jews in teaching. Negroes and Puerto Ricans have moved into the vacuum in the fast-expanding field of health services, but even there their strongest hold is on the jobs at the bottom of the scale, those that are the messiest and that pay the least. . . . The white civil servant becomes the 'enemy,' and the better union protectionism makes his job, the more intense the ghetto's resentment." [22]

Happiness

To the citizens of Cornwall-on-Hudson, happiness is the property tax. In 1965 the town's entire budget was $119,954, and levies against private homes paid for most of it. Then the Consolidated Edison Company, which sells most of its product in New York City, proposed to build a 162-million-dollar atomic power generator at Cornwall-on-Hudson. The tax from such an enterprise at current rates would bring in $500,000 to the town treasury—enough to put everyone's "borrowing relatives" on the public payroll. A few estate owners with fine properties overlooking the Hudson and its brooding Storm King Mountain sought to deny Consolidated Edison a building permit. The monstrous generating plant would intrude upon their scenery. Local businessmen and thrifty homeowners voted down these impractical objectors twenty to one in a referendum. "Con Ed has even agreed to paint its power lines green," rejoiced an ecstatic realtor. "Building lots that we couldn't sell for $2,000 now bring $15,000."

In the Mohawk Valley of Massachusetts, the town of Rowe is delirious. Its atomic power station already is in operation and the dividends are flowing in. "Where else can you have an $18,000 home and have annual real estate taxes of only $35?" asks businessman John H. Williams. "Why, you can pay them out of pocket money." It is the dream of every community to get the fancy industrial investment that will take the tax load off residential property, but nationwide residential construction runs five to three ahead of industrial, commercial, and utility construction. Furthermore, as the Philadelphia Federal Reserve Bank's Richard Epps reminds us, professional and commercial businesses, in contrast to industrial plants, ultimately require expensive public services. It takes a real bonanza to reverse the average cost-revenue ratio. The solution is an atomic generator in every locality.

Gloom

Three times in three years, Mr. and Mrs. Guy Hill of Portville, New York, offered to give their home town $80,000 to help it to finance a public overpass above a railroad crossing, if the community as a whole would match their gift with an appropriation of $70,000 so that the job could be done. In three successive referenda the voters rejected the offer. Despite the fact that thirteen jammed school busses daily negotiated the dangerous crossing while rail traffic was at its peak, the citizens, who include many parents, objected to the idea because it would raise their tax rate. The Hills have no children of their own.

The people of South Kingstown, Rhode Island, have a multi-million-dollar state university in their midst. Although blessed with intellect, they prefer cash. At an annual financial meeting of the town, they voted down a $25,000 appropriation for a sidewalk that would have enabled local children to go to school without walking in a busy street. The improvement would have raised the property tax rate less than 1 per cent for one year.

Geography

The jurisdiction of local governments are limited by their geography. These boundaries produce inequities in the public environment. School districts, water districts, sewer districts, police and fire districts are distinguished by wide disparities in the amounts and qualities of taxable real estate within their territories. Some districts are almost exclusively composed of low-cost, utilitarian structures in a mediocre state of repair. Other districts are high-class exclusive communities—too rich for the poor to get into. Since the quality of public services is directly related to the quality of real estate, some communities enjoy the very best in the way of schools, parks, streets, etc. Others are forced to get by with inferior everything. An American child's chances for future development and well-being depend not upon his nationality but upon his locality. There is no such thing as equality in the public environment because localities are primarily responsible for public services. There is no such thing as being born equal. It depends upon whether the address is good or bad. Good schools go with a good address, bad schools with a bad address—it is as simple as that. America is not a democracy when it comes to its public services. There is not even the semblance of equality between the public services of its Scarsdales and its Harlems.

This, of course, is one of the prime factors underlying segregation and the antagonisms that arise between social groups. Geographic boundaries are employed to freeze social inequities. As things now stand no amount of political oratory can raise enough revenue in a deprived community to put it on a par with those that have better real estate. There is a need, if the nation is to become a democracy in the future, for the Federal Government to give far greater grants-in-aid to states and localities than it does now. Along with these grants-in-aid there must be performance standards that oblige all states and localities receiving federal assistance to maintain minimum national standards in education, health, and welfare services.

It would make less sense for localities, or even states, to shift to the income tax because the geographical boundaries that produce inequities in their present property and sales tax bases would also apply to the income tax. Grants-in-aid could in no way jeopardize the local administration of local institutions but they could set minimum standards of decency in public service. They could begin to balance the most glaring of present imbalances.

In 1967 the U. S. Office of Education published a report showing that there was a per-student expenditure of $623 in the elementary and secondary schools of the United States. In Arkansas the expenditure per student was $441; in Mississippi $346. In New York State the average was $982.[23] Discrepancies within states are as great as between states. Neither Mississippi nor South Carolina has any state legislation which requires children to go to school at all. It is perfectly legal for a child to grow up a functional illiterate in those states; then when he cannot find a job as an adult, if he has any native intelligence, he moves to New York and goes on welfare. When states and localities ignore their public responsibilities it is not the duty of others to assume the burden—it is the duty of the national society and its Federal Government.

Economic Growth

On June 30, 1968, the United States completed its 23rd year of uninterrupted economic growth. It had closed the fiscal year with an increase of $56 billion to reach a new record of $822 billion. This meant goods and services of roughly $4,000 for every man, woman, and child in the nation. Behind economic growth that produces so much wealth lies the technological progress that substitutes inanimate energy for muscular work. Brain replaces brawn.

The urbanization process now going forward is technically and scientifically one of the great advances in human control over resources but its social impact is profoundly disturbing. Physicist-philosopher A. N. Whitehead states the case, "The major advances in civilization are processes that all but wreck the societies in which they occur." For the city to work, new social arrangements will be necessary. In 1920 there were 784,000 coal miners in the United States, and they produced an average of less than half a ton per hour. The Sunnyhill Mine near New Lexington, Ohio, can produce 1.6 million tons annually with a payroll of 67 men. The earnings of some Sunnyhill miners reach $19,000 a year. They operate automatic drilling machines which bore through coal seams at the rate of three feet per minute and deliver 266 tons per hour. Each machine is manned by three technicians stationed in a control cabin outside the mine. The borer itself is guided by a type of radar. Today there are fewer than 150,000 employed coal miners in America. Old mining communities in Appalachia are among the most depressed in the country. The half-ton-an-hour pick and shovel digger has no prospect of ever again getting on a payroll for that kind of work. While he and his dependents are piled on the human slag heap, GNP rises and the coal industry never was more prosperous.

America is committed to economic growth. This dedication is impersonal. It has no human bias. It does not spring from any altruistic desire to make life fuller, richer, happier for all. A deadly serious pursuit of technological power lies behind this commitment. Back in 1946 the Congress passed Public Law 304, sometimes known as the Full Employment Act. It declared that henceforth the Federal Government would "coordinate and utilize all its plans, functions, and resources" to achieve necessary economic goals. It created the authority by which the Federal Government subsequently came to use its vast purchasing power to beef up science, technology, and industry.

As the Federal Reserve Bank commented later, it was this policy which strengthened America's position when it became involved in the Korean War. "An important fact," said the Bank, "was driven home. If we were to maintain our position of strength in the cold war, yet still maintain the world's highest living standard, we must produce more, improve our productivity. In a word, we had to grow at the fastest possible sustainable rate." [24] Full employment really meant full employment of the most advanced technology and the resulting industrial capacity. It did not mean full employment of obsolete systems or obsolete people. It did not underwrite the full employment of all who wanted to work. It did assure industry that the government would stimulate the economy to keep factories with new technology busy. It did not assure people that they would be employed and it did not promise to teach them skills to make them employable. The aim of the Full Employment Act was to generate economic growth and industrial power. It was not a social welfare act. It was a cold war strategem.

In his Economic Report for 1954 President Eisenhower put the matter bluntly. "The United States," said the President, "is now engaged, and must be for some time to come, in an effort to build security forces adequate to deter and to strike back at aggression. These security-building efforts, and the parallel efforts to raise the defense potentials and the living standards of friendly people in other countries, are as much dependent on our industrial production as is the conduct of war itself. Success in them will depend in large part on the amount by which our national output is increased." In the interval since passage of Public Law 304, no national goal has been pursued more vigorously or consistently than the goal of military power through economic growth.

R & D

Technological progress and economic growth are stimulated by research and development, which introduce new efficiencies and make old systems obsolete. Dr. Alexander H. Flax, Assistant Secretary of the Air Force for Research and Development, reported in December, 1967, that "the Federal budget for research and development has experienced a steady and phenomenal growth over the past twenty-five years . . . the initiation of a massive space program added to a rising curve of cost for development and acquisition of ballistic missiles resulted in RDT&E growth rates in the neighborhood of 20 per cent per year. This trend, if it were to continue from the level of '66 for ten years, would result in a Federal RDT&E budget almost as large as the total budget of today by that time." [25] In 1966 the Federal Government spent $15 billion for research and development. Compounded at the rate of 20 per cent per year the figure could reach, as Secretary Flax had calculated, $92 billion by 1976. It was not likely to happen but at least the Pentagon was able to think in those terms. It could count on economic growth producing more federal revenues through the income tax.

While research produces new knowledge, that knowledge must be translated into hardware if plant capacity is to be expanded and full employment of that capacity is to be achieved. It is hardware-making even more than the initial R&D which results in "full employment." Once a critical mass has been achieved the research-to-hardware process becomes a chain reaction. There is, as Secretary Flax has said, "a price levied upon us if we wish to benefit from the fruits of this research; we must be prepared to pay the price of developing and manufacturing the machines, systems, and devices which research makes possible and this in turn calls for capital investments, the development of consumer needs and wants, and in some cases changes in consumer tastes." [26]

Secretary Flax was unequivocal. If military research and development are meaningful then the hardware must be made. An ABM in theory must become an antiballistic missile system even though the cost originally estimated by the Pentagon at $5 billion might, in the opinion of former Secretary of the Air Force, Senator Stuart Symington, go as high as $400 billion. Plant capacity to produce the hardware must be built by investing capital. And, of more than casual interest to the civilian consumer, his tastes in goods should be trained to coincide with what the new plants can turn out. The civilian value system should correlate with the military value system in the eyes of military planners. Viewed in this light the cures for urban ills most likely to be adopted should synchronize with the new industrial research-hardware system. Helicopters, armored cars, guns, handcuffs, and mace gas now being acquired by local police with federal assistance represent appropriate coordination.

In 1959 Paul H. Douglas, then a Senator from Illinois, reported that 721 retired military officers were employed by the top eighty-eight defense industries. In 1969 Senator William Proxmire of Wisconsin issued another report to show that the number of retired high-ranking military officers now working for the defense industries has tripled to 2,072. This trend, he stated, "represents a distinct threat to the public interest. . . . The easy movement of high-ranking military officers into jobs with major defense contractors and the reverse movement of top executives of major defense contractors into high Pentagon jobs is solid evidence of the military-industrial complex in operation." [27]

On March 10, 1969, Senator Proxmire took issue with this course of events. "I rise today to speak," said the Senator to his colleagues, "on a most serious matter. In my judgment the President and the Congress and, indeed, the country, have lost control over military spending . . . There is no adequate machinery, either in the executive or legislative branch to control the total amount spent or the way in which military funds are disbursed. This is especially the case with respect to contracting for major weapons systems . . . When former President Eisenhower left office, he warned against the danger of 'unwarranted influence, whether sought or unsought, by the military-industrial complex.' "

Senator Proxmire then went on to relate a conversation he had had with the Director of the Budget, Robert Mayo, who told him that only about 50 of the 500 persons on his staff were assigned to scrutinize the Defense budget although it accounts for about 80 per cent of the controllable items in the total federal budget—". . . that is," said the Senator, "items other than interest on the debt, pension and Social Security payments, and so forth, which are relatively fixed and not possible to cut except by major changes in legislation. . . . I think it is fair to say, therefore, that the Budget Bureau makes no adequate review of the military budget." [28]

This lack of review is due to a procedure common to all established executive departments and agencies, which is to concede the previous year's amounts as justified and to focus arguments for justifications on the new additions. The result is what has been described as "higher budgets, with past errors compounded year after year." As a correction in this procedure Senator Proxmire has proposed that "What we need . . . both at the Pentagon and elsewhere is 'zero-base' budgeting. The reviews should be made each year from the ground up. We should no longer accept uncritically last year's budget for any item, and then merely examine with some slight critical sense the added increment for the new year." [29]

In effect what Senator Proxmire said was that neither the Congress nor the Presidency ever takes a fresh look at the full spectrum of the nation's needs in order to match them against the long tally sheet of federal expenditures. Instead it is habit to pick up each year where the old year leaves off, making changes here and there but never a full reappraisal of priorities. The result is monumental spending on issues and commitments that seemed valid decades ago while those of present urgency are starved to death. The great bureaucracies are committed by their budgets to obsolete tasks while the Congress in its annual debates over public spending never gets back to zero-base. That is where it would have to start if it were to truly reassess the state of the nation in an urban-nuclear age when the great mass of its population lives in metropolitan areas and in which political negotiation rather than military combat is the only possible way to resolve international rivalries and still survive.

Reversal

Were it to apply its technological axe to man's most ancient fear—the fear of scarcity—the modern research-to-hardware industrial society could easily refute the Malthusian-Darwinian-Marxian thesis which lies at the heart of contemporary international conflict between political ideologies. A system designed for war in a world of scarcities could turn out to be the most effective instrument for peace in a world of abundance. Old Karl Marx knew only the most primitive experimental hand-operated model of what was to become the modern computerized industrial process. He lived during the initial coal-to-steam-power incubation period when massive numbers of cheap-waged muscle-work operatives drudged at awkward machines while only a few bosses enjoyed the rewards.

Marx could not imagine such a system ever being able to produce enough to reward adequately both capital and labor. His ideological opponents, being equally blind to the technological potential, agreed with his evaluation. But they found his remedy objectionable. In that smudgy tenement-blighted era of limited resources all agreed that only the fittest could survive as population increase put pressure on finite outputs. Capitalists and Communists alike were staunch Darwinians. A belief in scarcity was upheld by the political faithful of both worlds. All were true Malthusians. Their common assumptions about surplus populations and resource deficiencies forced them into separate ideological camps when it came to political solutions. The world was split down the middle.

Modern energy-resource industrial systems have refuted Marx as well as his critics. Regardless of political ideology both capital and labor now can be rewarded richly in any country where inanimate kilowatts replace human toil at routine drudgery. Mathematician-engineer-architect R. Buckminster Fuller has observed that if we were to take all the machinery of industrialization away from all the countries on earth and dump it in the ocean, within six months two billion humans would die of starvation and disease. On the other hand, Fuller declares, if we were to leave all the machinery in operation and instead take all the world's politicians and all their ideologies and send them into orbit around the sun, as many humans would go on eating as before and soon we would find better ways to take care of all humanity. Old systems of political thinking simply are not competent to administer the potentiality of modern technology. It would be just as possible in the future for "the fastest possible sustainable rate" of economic growth to emerge from the social processes of urbanization as from military build-ups. It would be a happier and safer world.

It is impossible to improve a city's economic mix, expand its physical shell, or revamp its institutions in response to national economic growth without boosting local public costs. Under present arrangements by which the responsibilities of different levels of government are divided, two approaches to better cities seem possible. One approach would be for the Federal Government to become universally responsible for paying the state and local costs of all education, health, and welfare services that result from the present research-to-hardware efforts to achieve the "fastest possible sustainable rate" of economic growth.

A second approach would be to reverse the present priorities by which the Federal Government emphasizes military procurement in its research-to-hardware contracts. Having already achieved a nuclear overkill capacity sufficient to annihilate all humanity it might shift its emphasis to procurement for a better public environment and thus make life better while it makes the economy stronger. For instance the Federal Government could become the central paymaster for all public construction and machinery required by the public environment: school buildings, hospitals, highways, mass transit systems, pollution control systems, and airports.

Neither of these approaches would alter the Federal Government's now fully established role as the prime generator of economic growth through its research-to-hardware commitments. Neither would interfere with the autonomy of states and localities. Their constitutional rights would not in the least be jeopardized by having their bills paid for them any more than the constitutional rights of General Motors or Boeing are threatened by having the Federal Government pay for the hardware they manufacture.

5
A Society of Responsibility

Urban Tensions

Neiman-Marcus of Dallas has teamed with Charles of the Ritz and the Great Southwest Corporation to banish anxiety from urban America. For the city woman who finds that daily tensions unravel her, these entrepreneurs have built a 2-million-dollar glass-enclosed restoration ranch called The Greenhouse. The decor is Texas seraglio with Muzak. Within its precincts patrons "seek out the perfection that is so beneficial for mind and body"—for $600 to $650 a week. "We're trying to counteract the pressure from the big cities," explains manager Mollie Porter Cullum. "It's the one place where there are no decisions to make." The guests, limited to thirty-six at a time, are attended by a staff of sixty-five who render "services that are truly Greenhouse."

"Each day," a brochure informs clients, "you don your delphinium blue exercise suit and the yellow rose of Texas terry robe to follow a prescribed schedule." Meals are served on Limoges china with "patterns varying by the hour and tablecloths turning from flowering prints to spirit-lifting tones of orange, gold, or green." Gradually, urban tensions ease as guests encounter "new approaches to the way you look, the way you feel . . . even to the way you think." Mrs.

Angus Wynne, Jr., whose husband is president of the Great Southwest Corporation, concedes that "$600 a week is a bunch, a real bunch," but, for those who do not have it, she confides, "They'll save up."

New approaches are precisely what are needed to ease urban tensions. Happily there is now a haven for those who "save up." For the rest there are problems.

Survival

Societies of living organisms existed before mankind itself evolved. While not all species live in groups, the phenomenon of aggregation is widely observed in nature. Even bacteria form colonies, prospering better in clusters than as individuals until they overpopulate or pollute their environment. Herds of reindeer, flocks of birds, swarms of insects, and schools of fish are familiar examples of animal societies. Interdependence results in higher survival ratios than living separately. To coexist within his own synthetic environment, urban man requires a society of responsibility.

The biological function of a society is the inclusion of the individual. Human beings have always had a better chance to avoid extinction by being gregarious than by being hermits. Today our chances are improved by being internationalist rather than isolationist—by integrating rather than by segregating. The urge to group, like physical characteristics, has remained within the genetic code inherited from more primitive forms of life. Over eons of time, the instinctual drive to socialize has found expression in the institutions of family, clan, tribe, and nation. These social artifacts are adaptive mechanisms that make it possible for members of groups to adjust to the environment as the environment itself is changed by human invention.

Now, because the environment undergoes accelerated and profound changes as a result of urbanization, the socializing instinct probes continuously for new cultural institutions

that will enable the individual to relate to others more effectively for their mutual survival. While old social relationships are not discarded, they erode. As urbanization pro-
gresses, both family and nation lose some of their effectiveness
as social groupings. Each must be supplemented by new institutions. Ultimately, each may be superseded by more
appropriate inventions. At the family level new more comprehensive social-security insurance mechanisms must take
over as the family itself proves to be inadequate. As the
econo-technic networks globalize, nations must be supplemented by institutions that promote international coexistence. Ultimately, nations will be superseded by a one-world
society, as territories become less meaningful relative to
worldwide institutional systems.

When families, clans, and tribes were adequate social aggregates, human relationships were more direct and personal.
The scale of association was smaller. Leaders could observe
the led and vice versa. Resources, being derived from natural
surroundings, were close at hand. The well-being of groups
was directly related to the territories they occupied. The
boundaries of social organization matched the boundaries of
resource production. There was on-site coordination between
the social groupings and their landscapes. Reciprocation between leaders and led was the heart and soul of feudal societies; each was related to the same piece of earth.

The sharing of a common territory and the resources it
possessed was the foundation of representative democracies.
The represented and the representative had a common
ground. United States Congressmen still represent geographic
territories because the representative system began in an
agrarian age. Theoretically our representatives do not represent institutions, which today are more meaningful aggregates of constituents than aggregations defined by place of
residence. All the people who reside in a congressional district may have far less in common than the same number of
people associated with the aerospace industry, or with the

welfare program of aid to dependent children. However, in reality, the representatives of representative government do represent institutions and interests but, because of the mythology of regional representation, the reality of institutional representation is denied—thus weak institutions and weak people are poorly represented, if at all. An urban democracy requires that all people be represented instead of all geographic areas. One-man-one-vote is not enough as long as some are more equally represented than others. Demands for direct participatory democracy arise from the discriminatory undemocratic practices of representative government, which represent people according to their places on the landscape rather than according to their places in society.

Representation

The Honorable Shirley Chisholm, Democrat, is the first Negro woman to be elected to Congress. Hers is a predominantly Negro and Puerto Rican district in the Bedford-Stuyvesant section of Brooklyn. Her people's problems are densely crowded slums, poverty, bad schools, and unemployment. Bedford-Stuyvesant has a population about the same as that of Denver, Colorado, but it has only one public high school. Legal action was required to create a congressional district within Bedford-Stuyvesant, which previously had been divided among other districts by gerrymandering. Congresswoman Chisholm was the first to be sent to Washington from the new district. She arrived in January, 1969, and requested to be assigned to the House Education and Labor Committee. The Democratic members of the House Ways and Means Committee assigned her to the Forestry and Rural Villages Subcommittee of the House Agriculture Committee.

Her constituents complained. "Shirley," they told her, "we don't grow hogs in this district. How did you get on that committee?" "I don't know where I'll end up," Congresswoman Chisholm exclaimed as she protested the assignment to a caucus of the Democratic Party, but she assured her constituents that they "will know they have a representative who won't sit back and take the system . . . It seems to me that it is time for the House of Representatives to pay attention to other considerations than its petrified, sanctified system of seniority, which is apparently the only basis for making most of its decisions." If she makes it, the Honorable Shirley Chisholm may find a way to make representatives representative, but it will not be easy. Now she is on the Veterans' Affairs Committee.

Urbanites rely for social relevancy upon legitimate status within institutional networks whose boundaries seldom coincide with those of political territories. A Congressman who represents a geographic district does not effectively represent a constituent whose company is headquartered in another state. Members of Congress who lose an election inadvertently prove this point by staying in Washington. When they do not return to their home districts to live, it is not because they are embarrassed. Rather, they have discovered that their own welfare has become more closely associated with industries and businesses with offices in the Capital than with the territories that once sent them to the Hill.

The more urbanized we become, and the more widespread and comprehensive the econo-technic networks become, the less representative is the agrarian system of representative government which is territorially defined. As a consequence, the unrepresented contituent feels a growing need for direct participatory democracy within his own organizational matrix. The labor unionist wants a direct vote to approve or reject contracts. Parents and students want to have direct influence on educational policy. The poor want influence within poverty programs. The voter who expects to vote Democratic wants to participate in the formulation of the party's platform, in the election of its committeemen, and in the nomination of its candidates. The churchgoer wants his church to be relevant to his daily life, rather than to moralize in Sunday detachment. The urge to become personally involved in decision-making increases as representation becomes less representative. Currently there is talk in state legislatures and in Congress about calling a constitutional convention. A prime topic for reconsideration at such a convention should be the present system of representation by geographic area. A serious debate on the subject might well convince the delegates that states and congressional districts are agrarian anachronisms in an age that finds most people dependent for their survival not upon a particular place but upon their status in the national networks of private and public enterprises. Representation by institutional and social status would be more meaningful than representation by geographic location.

Biologically the pressures for institutional change as evidenced by the revival of participatory democracy may be interpreted as efforts to create a society that is more responsive to the needs of individuals to be part of an effective group. When the individual feels shut out, his impulse is to change the system to make it more receptive. A genuine society of responsibility responds to this biological drive. The radical riots to force change, not to destroy the environment either physically or institutionally. In an advanced technological society, any genuine destruction of the environment would destroy the destroyer. All the resources that sustain the society are dependent upon that environment and its preservation.

The conservative who resists institutional change is as dangerous as any anarchist. It is the biological function of the environment to provide food, shelter, and security to the inhabitant. If some are in jeopardy because they are rejected by the system, then the system must be changed to include them and give them security. Resistance to change can only incite rebellion. For any society to remain viable, it must change to make accommodation for its people. For those who cannot "save up" there must be an alternative.

The rise of the European Economic Community and other international trade blocs is a step toward the dissolution of national sovereignty because national sovereignty severely restricts rational technological evolution and the social distribution of technology's benefits. The formation of worldwide international resource-making networks by the businessmen of all nations is a response to new technological opportunities for efficiency. These changes are also fundamentally responses to biological requirements, although they appear superficially to be economic and political. They are institutional responses to the most powerful of all psychic drives— the will to survive by having access to resources and meaningful status within the institutional networks. As the networks become global national political boundaries stifle technological efficiencies. Pressures arise to dissolve them.

The clamor in great cities for neighborhood control over school administration is an effort to achieve a comparable institutional adjustment on a micro-scale. Just as a nation is too small to coincide with the geographic scope of globalized econo-technic networks, a great city's centralized educational bureaucracy is too remote to respond to the needs of people in neighborhoods. On both the international macro-scale and the intraurban micro-scale, the individual must have a meaningful affiliation with life-giving, life-preserving institutions. Territorial boundaries are secondary. The only meaningful "territory" to urban man is his social status. Geographic place is meaningless; social place within the group is everything.

"Community control means only one thing," declares Kenneth W. Haskins, principal of the Morgan Community School, Washington, D. C. "The public institutions that serve a particular community should be controlled by it. In education, this movement has grown out of the failure of existing institutions to meet the needs of the children of the black community. The term 'racism' is often used in discussions of community control, and people recoil from it. . . . It means, for example, that a public school system that fails poor black children can be tolerated, while a public school system that fails white middle-class children cannot. The black community, therefore, has decided that it has to make the decisions about what can and cannot be tolerated for its children because society as a whole has largely failed . . ." [1] Direct participatory action by concerned black parents is the alternative to inaction by an unconcerned white bureaucracy. This is the logic of participatory democracy—the alternative to non-representative representation.

Since the people of Washington, D. C., are without political representation in the Congress of the United States, their only recourse is to exert whatever direct participatory pressures they can muster through their immediate institutions. The need is obvious as spelled out by a committee of the Congress which looked into the situation. "Your committee," declared the report, "has been informed that about 96,000 youngsters between the ages of 9 and 19 in 49,000 families live in circumstances approaching abject poverty . . . In one census tract of 9,800 people, for example, 72 per cent of all men and women over 25 lack high school education . . . The youth employment situation has serious dimensions in the District. For instance, most of the 6,000 young people registered with the District's Youth Offices of the U. S. Employment Service are without salable job qualifications. More than 75 per cent of them are high school dropouts." [2] Nobody cares but unrepresented people in the capital city of representative government.

It could be that the poor of the nation are not effectively represented because they are not rich. If only they were rich then representatives might pay attention to their poverty problems. Representative Lester L. Wolff of New York quoted a report in the *Congressional Record* that Standard Oil of New Jersey paid "six-tenths of one per cent in federal income taxes on a net income of $1,271,903,000 in 1962, increasing to five per cent federal income tax on $1,679,675,000 in 1965. It was a rate far below that of a widow with one child paying taxes on $1,500 in taxable income." [3] While Congressman Wolff tried to represent the widow, he was outvoted on tax reform by colleagues who took pity on poor Standard Oil of New Jersey. The fallacy of territorial representation was obvious. Some institutions get represented; some do not. For the unrepresented participatory democracy is an answer.

"Money," declares Jesse Unruh, California's Democratic powerhouse, "is the mother's milk of politics." [4] Drew Pearson said, "Anyone who yearns to be President must have, or know where to find it if he needs it, 5 million dollars just to win the nomination . . . Usually, the basic requirement for a House race is put at $50,000." [5] Stephen Horn writes, "In 1966, Richard M. Nixon renewed his campaign for the Presidency with one paid employee. By the time he had swept various 1968 Republican primaries and brought his triumphant organization to Miami Beach to secure his party's nomination, he had almost 150 paid employees and a $200,000 monthly payroll." [6] Apparently, confidence had grown among some that they would be represented.

Investigating the Eisenhower campaign of 1956, Senator Albert Gore of Tennessee found that the Rockefeller family contributed $152,604; the Du Pont family, $248,423; the Pittsburgh Mellons, $100,150; and the Sun Oil Pews put up $216,800. [6] As chairman of the tax-writing Senate Finance Committee, Senator Russell B. Long had apparently represented some of his constituents so well that when Senator Edward Kennedy challenged him for his job as Democratic Party Whip in the Senate, Long was able to get executives of six oil companies to urge an oil-state colleague to vote for him. [7] In this case, their influence was no greater than that of Eldridge Cleaver upon Ronald Reagan. Before long, the Senate chambers may ring with the direct participatory protests of petroleum company executives clamoring for "Oil Power."

Again we are back to a key concept that in an urban society the possession of a relevant place in the institutional network is the equivalent of land ownership in an agrarian society. Title to land gives a farmer social legitimacy. In an urban society, social legitimacy is expressed in institutional status. Parents who cannot influence school policy to the benefit of their children's education do not have institutional status. Within the synthetic environment of an urban civilization, any society with a sense of its biological responsibilities must synthesize new institutional structures that answer to contemporary needs.

"Our educational system, our system of local government, the civil service and the legal system are all now under critical examination because technology has made them obsolete. . . . Just as technology is revolutionizing industry, so it is outdating our political institutions as well." These are the reflections of a politician—Anthony Wedgewood Benn, Member of Parliament and Minister of Technology in Great Britain's Government.

"People want a much greater say," notes Minister Benn. "That certainly explains the student protests against the authoritarian hierarchies in some of our universities. Much of the industrial unrest—especially in unofficial strikes—stems from the resentment of workers and their sense of exclusion from the decision-making process . . . Even the Black Power movement is an indication that colored immigrants are not prepared to rely entirely on white liberals to champion their cause. All these tendencies are indicative of a general—and inevitable—trend away from authoritarianism and toward personal responsibility." [8] He was commenting about England—not the United States. Everywhere political representatives become increasingly detached from the represented. Because no single person, not even a king, commissar, or president, seems to be directly responsible for anything within the bureaucratic maze of a technological society, the individual demands the right to speak up when his interests are involved—even if no one is listening.

The resource-making, resource-assigning econo-technic networks now emerging must be matched by equally comprehensive social networks both within nations and between them. At present, two-thirds of humanity is not included within a viable social network. At present, minorities within industrially advanced nations are not socially included. The more sophisticated science and technology become, the more aggravated become the tensions within those forms of social aggregation that developed in simpler environments by which we are still linked. It is no wonder that the most remarkable achievements in technology are accompanied by the most fearful social outbursts from divorce at the family level to war among nations. For the most part, our social institutions and their behavioral codes are baggage carried over from a slower changing past. They are too inflexible for an era of rapid change; they are too rigid and simplistic for the new population aggregates that are pluralistic. As compensation for submitting to the discipline of the econo-technic bureaucracies, the individual demands a greater measure of security and personal freedom. Nations demand similar compensations when they relax their sovereignty in the interests of worldwide economic development and peaceful coexistence.

The individual in a pluralist urban society is a nonentity except as he is affiliated with a set of groups which in turn interact to make their constituents viable. As these institutions mutate some changes prove more adequate than others and they survive. The more remote from their constituents the representatives of representative government become, the more meaningful becomes participatory activity within all the institutions that circumscribe our lives. None but the poor can possibly have the greatest interest in programs to eliminate poverty. To the bureaucrats who administer them, poverty is a successful career. The insecurity of others is their security.

Poverty

The *Providence Evening Bulletin* investigated a Neighborhood Youth Corps summer project in Johnston, Rhode Island. Officially it was intended only for young people from disadvantaged poor families with less than $2,400 annual income. In reality it catered to middle-class families with incomes that averaged more than $5,000. Although federal guidelines specified that high school dropouts or potential dropouts should be employed so as to encourage them to finish school, it turned out that 42 per cent of the enrollees already were high school graduates—11 per cent were in college. The program was designed for slum youths from families which did not own either cars or homes. However 88 per cent of the parents owned cars while 70 per cent owned homes. One of the enrollees was the daughter of the town police chief. Four other town officials had offspring enrolled in the program. Meanwhile there were plenty of young people from poor families in Johnston who met every federal specification, but they were excluded from its benefits although they had been used as statistics to justify its approval. The town's chief educator, its superintendent of schools, was director of the enterprise, which paid him $200 a week in addition to his regular salary. It was an inspiration to the youth of Johnston to become educated.

Small town officials are not the only ones to throw away the rule book when it comes to poverty programs. Participating in a Youth Opportunity program, the U. S. Post Office Department hired 8,685 youths at $2.29 an hour as summer replacements for vacation postmen. The project was designed to help students in need "because of economic or educational disadvantages." After the summer was over, it turned out that 39 per cent of the summer jobholders had been selected from the patronage lists of Congressmen. Several of the appointees were sons or relatives of the lawmakers. When questioned about the matter, a Post Office spokesman observed, "Obviously, there was some abuse," but, he added, "it got the kids off the street, helped get them back to school and helped us." Washington's own poor had no representatives in Congress; they were not on the patronage lists. Among the lucky ones were a son and a niece of millionaire Senator Hiram Fong of Hawaii—a member of the Senate's Committee on Post Office and Civil Service.[9]

Upon looking at government poverty programs in general after they had been in operation for some time, New York's Senator Jacob Javits came to the conclusion, "We have substituted for the maximum feasible participation of the poor the maximum participation of politicians."[10]

Attitudes

When Congressman John J. Rhodes of Arizona asked his constituents in 1968 whether government spending should be increased, decreased, or maintained at prevailing levels, he learned that 54.4 per cent wanted a reduction in spending for poverty programs; 18.3 per cent wanted an increase; 22.5 per cent favored no change. Congressman Donald G. Brotzman of Colorado got a similar response when he made a poll. He told his constituents that "the National Advisory Commission on Civil Disorders recommends that the Federal Government substantially increase expenditures for anti-poverty and other social programs." Then he asked, "Do you approve?" A total of 64.1 per cent said "no"; 26.7 per cent said "yes"; the rest were undecided. When viewers of Station KOB-TV of Albuquerque, New Mexico, were asked, "Do you think Congress should cut back and completely re-examine the war on poverty?" a majority of 69.7 per cent said "yes"; 30.1 per cent said "no." When Congressman Brotzman asked his constituents, "Do you think more of our federal, state, and local resources should be channeled into law enforcement?" the response was 67.0 per cent in favor of more police; 19.3 per cent against; 13.6 per cent undecided or not responding.[11]

Who Are the American Poor?

If poor families are defined as those with total incomes of less than $3,000 per year, then 14.3 per cent of all American families are poor. The average annual income of these families was $1,650 in 1966. Who are these people? Where do they live? What is their social status? Why has technological progress bypassed them so that they do not share in the rewards of affluence? In 1966, the richest one-tenth of the American population received 29 per cent of all personal income. The poorest one-tenth received 1 per cent of all personal income.[12] Obviously they are only peripherally related to the total society. Their institutional connections are practically non-existent. As far as they are concerned, America is not a society of responsibility, and they are non-participatory.

An official tabulation by the U. S. Bureau of the Census shows that 26 per cent of all poor families are headed by females, whereas women head only 10 per cent of all other families. Just 15 per cent of the heads of poor families have finished high school while 59 per cent have not gone beyond the eighth grade. A majority of 87 per cent live in towns and cities while 13 per cent live on farms. Twenty-seven per cent of all poor families have no wage earner at all because no one is employable as a result of advanced age, illness, or other disqualification. Five per cent of the heads of poor families are temporarily unemployed while another 15 per cent have been out of work so long they are counted as not being in the labor force. This adds up to 20 per cent unemployed in addition to those 27 per cent who are not employable. Persons over age sixty-five are heads of 22 per cent of all poor families.

When it comes down to specifics, it turns out that the poor, in one way or another, are real socioeconomic basket cases. They are not plugged into the life-sustaining institutions of our urban society. What are called "families" in the statistics often are only fragments; so they do not even have the benefit of that agrarian-age welfare institution. Most of the heads of these statistical "families" are either too old, ill, or poorly educated, in a culture that emphasizes youth, robust health, and advanced education. A majority are mothers with dependent children who have the dual responsibility of earning a living and caring for their offspring at the same time in a society which seldom provides day care centers for the children of working mothers. Prostitution is a sometime solution. Society practically demands it, but not all can qualify for that. Some of the poor are discriminated against because they are Negro. Most are concentrated in cities where muscle work is not salable, yet they lack the education for other tasks. They are in a peculiar situation. They are accused by society of being lazy and unwilling to work, yet the same society which accuses them of laziness will not agree to have its government be the employer of last resort.

When a Gallup poll asked a cross section of Americans how they would react to a proposal "to guarantee enough work so that each family that has an employable wage earner would be guaranteed enough work each week to give him a wage of about $60 a week or $3,200 a year," the response was 79 per cent in favor; only 16 per cent opposed the idea; 5 per cent had no opinion. Despite these humane attitudes, the representatives of representative government have not been disposed to make Washington an employer of last resort except for themselves. When a deposed Congressman fails to make it with private industry after he has lost an election, there is always some executive agency of the Federal Government with an opening to fall into as a last resort. The Urban

Coalition, one of the most perceptive and respected associations of private economic leadership, has appealed to Congress to guarantee a job for everyone able to work but unable to find private employment. It has failed. *The Wall Street Journal* sees no reason for the Federal Government to carry the burden. "While most of the nation believes in help for the helpless," editorialized the *Journal,* "it also believes in the greatest possible degree of self-help and the greatest practicable dispersal of government powers." Self-help is a subscription to *The Wall Street Journal.* A 1963 survey of its subscribers showed that their median annual income is $16,521 and on the average each owns "9 suits (5 regular, $92 each; 4 lightweight, $71), 19 shirts ($6), and six pairs of shoes ($21)." Also many are said to "buy liquor by the case and cigars by the box."

For non-subscribers, how might the problem of poverty be solved? To be adequate, any solution would require comprehensive social action even though sometimes the causes are neither economic nor social. Old age, for instance, comes to everyone who does not die a premature death. Since one or the other is certain, only adequate comprehensive and compulsory health, accident, and retirement insurance for everyone could do the trick. A guaranteed job at a minimum decent annual wage is a must for all employables. For the unemployables, there should be automatic compensation. "More than half the poor," reports the *Washington Post,* "are either under 16 or over 65, and therefore not available for work." Vocational reeducation at any time of life would help those who are physically sound but who are junked by technological progress. Cyril D. Tyson, New York's Commissioner of the Manpower and Career Development Agency, estimates that a ten-year effort to train and place 565,500 persons who have been on relief rolls, high school dropouts, or hard-core unemployed would reduce city welfare costs and increase tax revenues by more than $7 billion. A guaranteed annual income should be available to all dependent mothers and children whose fathers and husbands have died or abandoned them. Decent living allowances and institutional care should be the birthright of all who are born mentally or physically handicapped. Blessed with the material affluence of America, a genuine society of responsibility could do no less.

While powerful influences in urban America run counter to such concepts of social responsibility they are already widely accepted and in operation for most of the upper and middle classes. Once implemented, comprehensive all-risk guaranteed income and hospitalization plans are seldom thought of by the public as welfare programs but that is what they are. Every worker on Social Security, every participant in a retirement fund, every executive whose future is secured by below-cost stock options with automatic capital gains opportunities shares in a welfare system. Practically all Americans are on welfare except the poor. Welfare is the heart and soul of the fringe benefit programs widely acclaimed by the employees of industry and government. The whole of society pays the premiums for these benefits either through direct taxation or hidden in the higher costs of commodities. To finish the job by including every American whether rich or poor in these comprehensive insurance schemes would add very little to the total costs now accepted. Welfare programs paid for by private manufacturers and passed on to consumers now amount to 11.4 per cent of total gross payroll costs.

In 1966, a total of 62 per cent of all private and public employees were covered by employer-sponsored life insurance and death benefit programs; 73 per cent had hospitalization coverage. Sixty-four per cent of the labor force had unemployment insurance coverage in 1967.[13] America has a well-developed welfare program for its well-fed, well-educated, employed majority. It just does not have such a program for those who need it most.

Health, education, and welfare services are the direct

measure of a society's sense of responsibility. These services accounted for 42.5 per cent of all public expenditures by all levels of government in 1967. Trust fund expenditures are, of course, included in these figures. In 1967, expenditures for these services amounted to 13.1 per cent of gross national product. Social insurance, chiefly retirement payments under Social Security and other trust funds, accounted for 37 per cent of the total bill. Education, paid for chiefly out of taxes, ranked second with 35 per cent. Health and medical care, paid for out of trust funds and taxes, accounted for 16.1 per cent. The great preponderance of these expenditures went to help the not-poor, who received payments and services under insurance plans. Most public expenditures for education went to the not-poor middle class, which not only has the most children in school but keeps them there longer at public expense—usually through college.

Among the persons most heavily subsidized by public welfare programs are physicians, lawyers, and college professors who get the most prolonged and costliest educations. Grade school dropouts get the least public service unless they end up on welfare to balance things out. Public handouts to the very poor account for only 8.9 per cent of all social insurance and tax-financed expenditures on health, education, and welfare. Since the very poor are 14.3 per cent of the population, they do not even get their proportionate share of the social inputs.[14] They are the ones who should complain loudest about too much spending on welfare programs. As it is, those who benefit most from public welfare programs are the first to denounce the extravagance. They apparently assume there is a difference between consumer-paid benefits and taxpayer-supported public benefits. It is a nice case of rationalization which reveals how poorly informed the general public is regarding present welfare programs and the basic ecological function of comprehensive welfare systems in an urban society where the individual has no direct access to life-sustaining resources as he did in the age of hunters and gatherers.

Model

Just before he stepped out of office, former Secretary of Defense Clark M. Clifford addressed representatives of private industries belonging to the National Security Industrial Association. "This audience," said the Secretary, "is as close as one can ever come to assembling the leading representatives—in and out of uniform—of what General Eisenhower once referred to as the military-industrial complex . . . Inevitably there is danger when one is talking about the expenditure of 40 or 60 or 80 billion dollars a year. I submit that the Department of Defense, a Department which consumes 9 per cent of the gross national product of our nation, a Department which employs four and one-half million Americans, has a deep obligation to contribute far more than it has ever contributed before to the social needs of our country."

Secretary Clifford then went on to describe in detail how the Department of Defense came to an awareness of social needs by being the nation's single largest housing contractor, the operator of its greatest hospital-medical complex, its single most important educational institution—"We train military people in 1500 separate skills, and our schools for service children are in 28 countries around the globe"—and America's most successful stimulator of new jobs in ghettos —"More than 50 of our major Defense contractors have launched specific projects . . . such as in the Watts area of Los Angeles and the Roxbury area of Boston." The Secretary then closed his address by appealing for cooperation between industry and government to solve domestic social problems. "We now have a military-industrial team with unique resources of experience, engineering talent, management and problem-solving capacities, a team that must be used to help find the answers to complex domestic problems as it has found the answers to complex weapons systems."

Secretary Clifford has hit upon an idea with tremendous potentialities. Were every citizen drafted into the defense establishment's sub-culture at birth he would, without any further qualification, belong to a society of responsibility. The military and their dependents are all provided with excellent comprehensive insurance coverages which could serve as models for the total nation. Military posts either provide their own low-cost housing or pay rent supplements to needy personnel living off-base. Either they support their own schools from kindergarten to West Point and Annapolis, or federal aid is extended to public schools and universities attended by the military and their dependents. "We must not place the children of the military in a second-class category by giving them a second-rate education," asserts Congressman Robert O. Tiernan of Rhode Island. The state's best public schools are in districts receiving federal aid as "impacted areas."

Complete medical and hospitalization coverage is extended to military personnel and dependents. Retirement annuities are earned after twenty years of service. Being a national institution, rather than a geographic area, the defense establishment enjoys representation by representatives from all the states. Thus it has made the transition from the agrarian-territorial past into the technological-institutional present. It is socially progressive, having desegregated its own facilities. Around its bases, it has persuaded landlords to rent apartments in the same buildings to white and black alike while they are in uniform.

The "military-industrial complex" has responded to pleas to redeem the ghetto. General Motors has hired over 21,700 "hard-core unemployables" and trained them to be reliable workers. Ford and Chrysler have done the same with more than 9,300 and 5,800 respectively. Wayne Grimm runs a "hard-core" program for Chrysler. When he asked a man

who had been on the job for seven months "what difference it made," he was told, "My kids have got good shoes.
We eat better. My wife thinks I'm a hero." Grimm says,
"You can't ask for much more." Spokesman for GM's program report that the percentage of hard-core workers who
stay with the firm is "just about the same as all persons
hired"—about 76 per cent. Economist Sylvia Porter says
1,500,000 hard-cores remain to be given a chance.

The armed services' PX system is the most accommodating
discount merchandising chain in existence. Their recreation
facilities are choice. According to federal accountants, the
innkeepers at Fort Gordon, Georgia, are about tops. During
a Masters Golf Tournament at nearby Augusta, they offered
single rooms to visiting brass for 40 cents and family quarters
for $2.50 a day while downtown hotels charged $20. In addition the military innkeepers offered free transportation to
and from the links. It was a successful pilot study in patron
response to nationalized mass transit. In all these imaginative
ways the defenders of the free-enterprise state have demonstrated how easy it is for the public to sustain comprehensive
social services without undermining the system. Only a
cynic would accuse the professional defenders of the capitalist system of having established the world's most comprehensive socialist society for themselves.

Analysis

While poverty in urban America wears many faces, the fact
remains that it is not due to a shortage of resources. There
is plenty to go around to afford a minimum level of
decency for everyone no matter how handicapped. Between
1960 and 1967, gross national product increased at a rate
that was slightly more than three times the birth rate. Populations averaged an annual increase of 1.4 per cent while
GNP in constant dollars increased at an average rate of 4.6
per cent—a net rate of increase of 3.2 per cent per capita.

In 1968 the record was even better. The birth rate declined
to 1.0 per cent while GNP increased in constant dollars by
5 per cent—a net rate of increase of 4.0 per cent per capita.[15]
If all the poor families in the nation, who numbered 7,000,-
000, had received cash subsidies averaging $1,350 to bring
their average incomes of $1,650 up to the poverty border-
line of $3,000, the total cost would have been $9.5 billion.
That would have been 1.1 per cent of the 822-billion-dollar
GNP for the fiscal year 1968-69. As Clark Clifford said in
1968, "The Department of Defense now consumes 9 per cent
of the gross national product of our nation." If just slightly
over 1 per cent of the 1968-69 GNP had been transferred as
an outright subsidy to the poor families of America, their
most wretched conditions would have been relieved. Put another way, if just one-fifth of the 56-billion-dollar *increase* in
GNP which occurred in 1968-69 had been assigned to the
poor, the same goal would have been attained. Obviously, the
problem of poverty in America is not financial—it is in-
formational and psychological.

Considering America's popular image of itself as a civilized
society, it would be hard to believe that the majority who
each year earn 103 to 104 per cent of the previous year's income (in constant dollars) would not be willing to grow
richer at the rate of $2\frac{1}{2}$ to $3\frac{1}{2}$ per cent per capita per year
rather than 3 to 4 per cent, if by doing so the worst poverty
could be abolished. Put another way, if the most affluent
one-tenth of American society which receives 29 per cent of
all money income were willing to take a cut of $\frac{1}{29}$, then the
average annual income of the poorest one-tenth of the population, which receives 1 per cent of all money income, could
be doubled.[16]

As it is, in the six years between 1960 and 1966, the share
of the nation's total money income which went to the wealthiest tenth increased from 27 to 29 per cent while the share
which went to the poorest tenth of the nation's families remained unchanged at 1 per cent. The rich grew richer while

the poor remained poor and, for the most part, invisible except for an occasional exposure on TV. A television producer with a private income spends $80,000 a year to live in New York and complains, "I'm broke"; so maybe there is no more slack at the top than there is at the bottom. Tuitions for his children in private schools cost $6,000 a year, taxes on his brownstone $4,000; the boatyard charges $1,500 to store and repair his sailboat. "I am still as far from the glamorous kind of New York life as a steel worker," he asserts. "The only way out is to inherit money, or to have an important corporate job with stock options and complicated expense and tax procedures"—from the resident of a fashionable midtown ghetto that's telling it like it is.

Subsidies

In 1967, the Federal Government paid out $6.8 billion in subsidies to affluent segments of society because their activities were said to be in the national interest. Almost two-thirds of these direct subsidies, $4.2 billion, went to farm landowners and operators. (The Department of Agriculture spent an additional $2.4 billion on other public services to farmers while allocating one-half billion in food stamps and surplus commodities to the poor and to schoolchildren's lunches.) In the same year, the average hourly wage paid by farmers to their own hired laborers was $1.12½ an hour. Only 13 per cent of all farm workers have jobs calling for at least 250 days of work. While it guarantees the prices of commodities to assure a profit to producers, the Federal Government does not require farmers to pay the minimum living wage of $1.44 an hour to their hired hands. To make $3,000 a year a laboring man must receive a minimum wage of $1.44 an hour 8 hours a day, 5 days a week for 52 weeks in the year.

Had the $4.2 billion in agricultural subsidies been paid to America's poor instead of to its most successful landowners, the income of 44 per cent of all the poor families in the entire nation could have been raised to the minimum $3,000 per year level. It is doubtful if any additional taxes would have to be paid by anyone to eliminate poverty in America. The task would require a shift in the ways just a small portion of present revenues are spent. It is a question of priorities rather than a question of more money. As yet poverty is not recognized as a social responsibility. The individual is blamed if he does not make it regardless of how he might be handicapped. "It's American—the American-Protestant ethic —to be aga; ,t giving money for doing nothing," observed Wilbur J. Cohen, former Secretary of Health, Education, and Welfare. "I don't think that it is a case of money today. It is the psychological barrier." Yet the largest subsidies to the largest agricultural enterprises are payments precisely for "doing nothing." Maybe present priorities have nothing to do with the "Protestant ethic." The human herd of America's twentieth-century technological society may be responding to its most primitive paleolithic emotions—favoring those who are already "in" and resisting with fear and persecution those who are "out." Despite its astonishing affluence, the nation has a hangup about scarcity.

Various proposals have been made that would take the administration of poverty programs out of politics and away from public welfare departments by turning the job over to the Internal Revenue Service's computers. In this way large portions of welfare budgets which are consumed by chiselers and by the salaries of case workers and their hierarchy of supervisors could be saved so that the legitimate poor would get more mileage out of present appropriations. These proposals are known by different names such as "credit income tax," "income maintenance," "guaranteed annual income," and "negative income tax." They vary in detail but the purpose of all of them is to raise the incomes of the desperately poor to the most elementary humane level.

One of the first of such proposals, the negative income tax, was conceived by Dr. Milton Friedman, a leading conservative economist, president of the American Economic Association in 1966 and an advisor to both President Richard Nixon and Senator Barry Goldwater. "Most of the things we do now in the name of welfare help the 'not poor' at the expense of the poor," explains Professor Friedman. As social security institutions are now developed, most private and public benefit schemes are geared to the middle-class wage earner rather than to the unemployed, the uneducated, and the handicapped. Local Community Chest Funds, for instance, support activities that for the most part serve the middle class through established churches, clubs, and societies rather than the very poor, who often lack such affiliations. When the United Fund of Rhode Island was asked what it could do for a crippled 72-year-old man living alone and trying to exist on $57 monthly from Social Security and $14.50 from the state's public assistance funds, it recommended that he "join a golden-age club."

Professor Friedman suggests that we do away with sham poverty programs that pretend to serve the poor but which too often are the dream boats of their promoters and the bureaucrats who administer them. The negative income tax would eliminate, Dr. Friedman says, ". . . the present ragbag of measures directed at the same end, the total administrative burden would surely be reduced." He has estimated that the administrative costs of present welfare programs eat up $4 for every $1 that gets to needy recipients. The politicians and bureaucrats whose hands are in the pockets of poverty programs would no longer be able to use the poor as an excuse for promoting their own welfare.

Table 1 illustrates how the negative income tax would work. The table assumes a family of four—the parents and two children—each entitled to $600 in personal exemptions according to present income tax legislation. Another $600 is allowed as a "standard deduction." Total deductions thus equal $3,000. If a family were to earn $3,000, which is the poverty income borderline, it would pay no tax under present laws. If, however, the family were poor and earned only $2,000 no tax would be paid but the family would lose an exemption credit of $1,000. In this case, Dr. Friedman's plan proposes that one-half the difference between the $3,000 exemption and the $2,000 income, or $500, be paid to the family by the Internal Revenue Service as a negative or reverse income tax.

TABLE 1

HOW THE NEGATIVE INCOME TAX WOULD WORK

Gross Income (Family of 4)	Tax	Subsidy	Net Income	
$4,000	$140	....	$3,860	
3,500	70	....	3,430	
3,000	...	....	3,000	
				(cut off poin
2,500	...	250	2,750	
2,000	...	500	2,500	
1,500	...	750	2,250	
1,000	...	1,000	2,000	
500	...	1,250	1,750	
0	...	1,500	1,500	

Economist Friedman thinks that this subsidy would help to rescue the destitute, yet not encourage any able person to be an idler. If this program had been in effect in 1966 it would have cost the Federal Government $4.25 billion as compared to the $4.4 billion it spent anyway on public assistance programs that did not assist most of the people who needed help because the administering bureaucracies, Federal, state, and local, consumed so much of the appropriation. If both the regular public assistance and farm subsidy programs had been discontinued that year, the $9.6 billion spent on them would have been just exactly enough to have furnished a 100 per cent guaranteed family income of $3,000 for every American. The politics of welfare raises the costs of public assistance while failing to do the job which could be done without any additional public spending. It is simply a question of who should get the money in a society of responsibility.

In August, 1969, President Nixon sent a message to Congress containing what Representative Clarence J. Brown of Ohio called "the most dramatic proposals in more than 30 years pertaining to the welfare system of this nation." [17]

"The present welfare system," said the President, "has failed us—it has fostered family breakup, has provided very little help in many States and has even deepened dependency by all-too-often making it more attractive to go on welfare than to go to work." Mr. Nixon then proposed ". . . that the Federal Government pay a basic income to those American families who cannot care for themselves in whichever State the live." Other notable ideas were contained in this message such as recommendations for "a major expansion of job training and day-care facilities . . . uniform Federal payment minimums for . . . the aged, the blind and the disabled . . . a plan for a system of revenue sharing with the States to help provide all of them with necessary budget relief."

The President observed further that "By breaking up homes, the present welfare system has added to social unrest and robbed millions of children of the joy of childhood . . ." Also ". . . by widely varying payments among regions, it has helped to draw millions into the slums of our cities." [18] The full message indicated that Mr. Nixon has been alerted as to how badly our society has failed thus far to respond responsibly to the needs of our weakest members. Nevertheless the rhetoric of his analysis was far from being matched by recommendations for adequate funding. Phrases and dollars did not balance. For instance, it was proposed that for the typical "welfare family"—a mother with three dependent children and no outside income—the basic national minimum payment should be $1,600 although $3,000 has long been considered the absolute bottom required for health and decency. No welfare program at all was recommended for single adults not handicapped or aged, nor for married couples without children. Yet there was no proposal that the Government should become an employer of last resort for the unemployed.

The Urban Coalition, headed by former Secretary of Health, Education and Welfare, John W. Gardner, praised the Nixon proposals "for moving to correct serious deficiencies in the current system." But it urged that they be strengthened by raising the levels of the low federal minimum payments and by creating job programs that would give employables an opportunity to work.[19]

The New York Times; 8/15/69

It is understandable that some of the strongest opposition to guaranteed full employment and automatic income supplements comes from professional welfare workers and administrators. They would become superfluous. The U.S. Department of Welfare estimates that under the present system, the number of people on public assistance is 25 per cent of the total population whose income is below the poverty level, and half the number that would be eligible under federal welfare regulations. To make certain that their own salaries are not jeopardized, case workers systematically withhold information from their clients which would enable them to qualify for more aid. For persons able to work but without employable skills, Secretary of Labor George P. Shultz proposes a work program comparable to the G. I. Bill of Rights. Under the Shultz plan, school dropouts and others without training would get a job-training credit that would pay for their maintenance and tuition while they acquired a skill.

Even though present welfare programs including Medicaid reach only a fraction of the nation's poor their cost in federal funds alone was $4.4 billion in 1967. If all the poor were treated even according to present inadequate standards, the costs would double to at least $8.8 billion in federal monies and perhaps as much in state and local outlays. A minimum guaranteed income, or a negative income tax plan, plus a full-employment insurance program would cost less and eliminate the red tape of the welfare system with its excessive overhead of middle-class bureaucrats.

When Congressman William V. Roth, Jr., Republican of Delaware, was elected to the House for the first time in 1966, he tried to find out how many assistance programs there are to which the Federal Government contributes. To his surprise he discovered that the Executive branch, which administers these programs for the poor, as well as for million-dollar farm and shipping corporations, spends $20 billion annually on 1,090 programs, only 530 of which were listed in the best official compilation he could find up to the date of his study. Congressman Roth learned that ten cabinet-level departments and fifteen or more agencies operate federal assistance programs and no one, even he, knows the whole story.[20]

In May, 1968, over a thousand professional economists from 125 universities and colleges signed a statement endorsing "a national system of income guarantees and supplements." At about the same time twenty-six prominent businessmen, including E. Sherman Adams, senior vice president of First National City Bank, called for a national "system of income maintenance" to combat poverty. "The time has come," the businessmen declared, "to bring all of our citizens into full participation in the nation's economy and to provide adequately for those who, through no fault of their own, cannot participate."

The ultimate purpose of all comprehensive social insurance, educational, and full-employment programs is to break through the circle of poverty which surrounds an unnecessarily large segment of the American population. Sociologists are finding in their research that more and more children whose grandparents are also drawing public assistance are

coming onto the welfare rolls. More than 40 per cent of the
parents whose children receive "Aid for Dependent Children" funds themselves had parents who received welfare
checks. Assemblyman Stanley Steingut, chairman of New
York State's Joint Legislative Committee on Child Care
Needs, says that present programs are a "self-defeating"
failure for 500,000 children in the aid-to-dependent children
category and are "imprisoning them forever in the slum."
That is for New York State alone.

The growing concentrations of the poor in neighborhoods
of their own in big cities lead to effective isolation of poor
families from those who enjoy more successful existences.
The youngest of the poor, raised in these circumstances, learn
only the customs and folkways of social rejects. They learn to
apply for welfare but not how to qualify for employment.
Their schools are usually inferior, and public officials, including the police, who come in contact with them treat them
as delinquents. As psychologists would expect, a common result is delinquency. A contemporary slum is a prep school
where all may major in the culture of poverty.

Professor Earl R. Rolph of the University of California,
author of *The Credit Income Tax*, read a prepared statement
before the House of Representatives in the summer of 1968.
"If people are to break out of the poverty trap, their children, to take one large group, must have a sufficiently high
quality of home care including adequate diets, medical attention, and decent housing to permit them to perform effectively in school. If parents are provided with more ample
financial means, they can provide for their children more
effectively and many more of these children can then break
out of the vicious circle of poverty." [21]

Health

Dr. Arthur Bushel, Acting Health Commissioner of New
York, declares that poverty is the third leading cause of death

in his city. "The basis for this statement," says Dr. Bushel, "is that if we were able to achieve for our low-income districts the same death rates which we observe in the high-income districts the savings in human lives would be equivalent to eliminating the third leading cause of death." [22] The inequalities of medical services in America have long been recognized at the highest political levels. A quarter of a century ago in 1945, President Harry S. Truman remarked, "Benefits of modern medical science have not been enjoyed by our citizens with any degree of equality . . . Nor will they be in the future—unless Government is bold enough to do something about it." The President was thinking, of course, of the Federal Government, which alone could help to establish more uniform services across the nation by counterbalancing with all-inclusive prepaid health insurance programs the inequalities due to incomes and social status.

President Nixon's Secretary of Health, Education, and Welfare, Robert Finch, has shown signs that he would favor an enlightened comprehensive program of national health care such as that envisioned by former President Truman. But today it is just as strongly opposed by the American Medical Association as it was back in 1945. The AMA wants the free market and ability to pay to determine who gets what kind of medical care at what price. Health care to the AMA is a commodity to be purchased by those who will pay the most for it. It is not a human right available to all in a society of responsibility. The AMA tells the press that doctors will serve the truly indigent, if need be without charges, but genuine medical care is a joint responsibility of physicians and hospitals. As every sick person has learned, it is impossible even to get into a hospital or the examination rooms of many physicians without proof of ability to pay. Under present medical procedure, fiscal health is examined before physical health. That, in part, is why poverty, as Dr. Bushel says, is a major cause of death.

This is not an oversight—it is the system as evidenced by

the AMA's reaction to Secretary Finch's nomination of Dr. John H. Knowles to be the nation's most important medical officer—the Assistant Secretary of Health and Scientific Affairs. As director of the Massachusetts General Hospital of Boston Dr. Knowles came to know the inadequacies of modern health care in a great city. Frequently he spoke in opposition to policy positions of the AMA. He emphasized the need for more preventive medicine, and he declared that social and economic blocks prevent adequate health care for all. He noted that private medicine does too little for the poor and the aged. He advocated more federal aid for hospitals, lower hospital and doctors' fees, and he favored universal comprehensive health insurance for all Americans. Before a Senate subcommittee he declared, "I do believe in comprehensive prepaid health insurance for all Americans on a public and private basis. If the private basis will not do it, then I think the Federal Government has got to do it." On another occasion he said that the present Medicaid program has not provided quality standards or extended service. It is, he stated, "one of the largest abortions ever produced by a central authority." [23]

To the AMA such statements are a threat to its free floating-price system which gives each patient the freedom to decide how much his life is worth when he is sick. Even the affluent patient with Blue Cross and Blue Shield coverage does not know where he is at, for such insurance only guarantees down payments beyond which physicians and hospitals may add to their fees what the market will bear. The Blue Cross-Blue Shield insurance systems are not true "comprehensive prepaid health insurance," such as Dr. Knowles advocated. They are neither comprehensive nor fully prepaid. They establish the patient's credit rating and they have low cut-off points. A person with a serious prolonged illness soon exhausts his Blue Cross-Blue Shield credit. The AMA opposes genuine across-the-board prepaid comprehensive insurance because it would put a ceiling on all medical fees and services. The AMA declares that this would reduce quality but the Department of Defense and the Veterans' Administration operate hospitals with fixed fee personnel. They are usually the first place that eligible patients go when they need medical attention. Members of Congress and the President himself as Commander-in-Chief patronize this system, which the AMA calls "socialized medicine."

The nomination of Dr. Knowles to be Assistant Secretary of Health and Scientific Affairs brought out the big guns of the AMA to shoot him down. With the help of Senator Everett Dirksen of Illinois, Senator John Tower of Texas, and Representative Bob Wilson of California their mission was accomplished. Senator Tower is chairman of the Senate Republican Campaign Committee, and Congressman Wilson heads the House Republican Campaign Committee. These campaign fund managers rely heavily upon the AMA and its affiliated organizations to replenish their coffers. It has been estimated that the AMA membership and their associates put up an estimated $2 million in 1967 and 1968 to promote the elections of President Nixon and congressional candidates of both political parties who they thought would uphold their point of view on matters of public health. The AMA's Political Action Committee (AMPAC) alone spent $681,965 to support candidates it believed would hold the line against truly effective Medicare and Medicaid. It was a good hunch and a good bargain. With the defeat of the Knowles nomination it looked as if political campaign spending in the right place had staved off adequate federally supported comprehensive prepaid medical care for all Americans for at least another presidential term. When the chips were down, congressional representatives who had been supported by AMPAC remembered whom they represented.

Coming as it did over five months after the new administration had assumed office the Knowles decision, according to United Press International, was "viewed by some as the climax of a struggle between Republican conservatives and liberals for control in the Nixon Administration." Medical care, aid to the poor, public school education, civil rights, peace in Vietnam, world disarmament, government-sponsored open housing and guaranteed employment for everyone—all issues which the Johnson Administration had failed to address itself to beyond tokenism seemed destined to get a similar brush-off from its successors. American society seemed headed for another four years of drift by its political leadership while accelerated polarization continued to set faction against faction. The significance of urbanization as a resource-creating ecological process seemed to be completely missed by those in the most powerful positions to make the nation not only an affluent society but one with a conscience and a sense of cohesion as well. The political mind still believed in scarcity even with annual GNP climbing at a 4 to 5 per cent rate in constant dollars.

Not until 1966 did medical care under the Social Security insurance system become available to persons over sixty-five. Even then what is called "Medicare" covered only about 35 per cent of the health needs of the elderly. Prolonged terminal illness is frequent among them and the most costly, yet Medicare is limited to 90 days of hospitalization per illness plus a lifetime reserve of an additional 60 days. If those who develop a hospitalizable chronic illness neither die nor recover within the time limit Social Security cuts them off. The poorest end up in state mental institutions where the cost of care per patient is less than in hospitals because less care is rendered. It is an economical technique of human warehousing devised by a mentally ill society.

A presidential committee reported in 1967 that 7,000 new patients each year develop chronic uremia. About 1,000 are kept alive either by kidney transplants or by use of artificial kidney machines. The rest die because they cannot afford to rent the machines. A uremia patient in New York City spends two nights a week in the hospital hooked to a dialysis apparatus. "Due to this artificial cleansing of the blood," says

Senator Vance Hartke of Indiana, "he can live the rest of the time fairly normally, and continues his work . . . The cost of his in-hospital treatment is in excess of $300 per week and $100 additional for special nurses. Because of this, the patient called this dialysis treatment 'survival for the wealthiest.'" In the Washington metropolitan area, 300 persons annually need an artificial kidney to stay alive. But, according to an official of the National Kidney Foundation, only about ten are treated on dialysis machines in hospitals. Eight others have equipment at home. All together the hospitals in New York City and Westchester County have facilities for only sixty-six patients.[24]

In 1968 the escalating costs of the Vietnam war had unbalanced the federal budget. Both President Johnson and the Congress pressed for reductions in federal services to civilians to make up some of the deficit. During the same week in September, the Senate voted to cut back $200,000,000 in federal medical and hospital aid for the poor, and it slashed $500,000,000 from federal grants to states under Medicaid for the not-poor who are classified as "medically indigent" but otherwise self-sustaining. Having accomplished this thrift it proceeded to increase by $960,000,000 its appropriation for farm price support payments beyond the $3,274,539,000 previously budgeted.

When medical researchers held a conference at which federal cuts in medical subsidies were discussed, some thought research should be spared while the patient services should take the full reduction. Dr. H. Bentley Glass, a geneticist and academic vice-president of the State University of New York at Stony Brook, was reported to have said it would be better to reduce outlays for health care than to cut the flow of basic knowledge. The value of medical knowledge which is not extended to the patient apparently was not discussed.

The elderly and the poor are not the only ones who experience a gap in health care. The Selective Service report of 1967 showed that 28.5 per cent of all draftees examined were physically disqualified. Another 9.3 per cent were mentally disqualified, and 1.4 per cent were rejected for both physical and mental deficiencies. Alabama, Arizona, and Mississippi led all states in disqualified draftees with percentages of 50.8, 49.8, and 50.6 respectively. Oklahoma, North Dakota, and Montana had the best records with percentages of rejects running 22.8, 24.0, and 26.7 respectively.[25] Since men of draft age are in the prime of life, it is apparent that a need for more adequate medical attention manifests itself long before age sixty-five, when Medicare begins.

The relationship between poverty and poor medical care is evident in a Harvard University Press study by O. W. Anderson, P. Collette, and J. J. Feldman. It shows that in 1958 families with annual incomes of $7,500 or more had median gross medical charges of $256. Families with annual incomes below $2,000 had median gross charges for personal health services of $59. Not only did the low-income families have inferior care but the care they did get amounted to a larger proportion of their incomes. For low-income families, the lesser charges for inferior care amounted to 13.0 per cent of their incomes. For the high-income families, the greater charges for superior care amounted to only 3.9 per cent of their incomes.[26]

If society were to regard the man-made environment ecologically, it would employ each advancement in science for human betterment. After all, medical research is almost totally dependent upon either public funds or tax-exempt foundation spending. Thus the public pays for a progressive technology in medicine but only those with adequate personal funds can afford the knowledge when it becomes deliverable. More meaningful than the theatrics of heart transplants would be the extension of routine medical care to all who need it. There is something morbid about an emphasis upon techniques that only a very few can afford while thousands die for lack of routine care. A society of responsibility would be as interested in the application of knowledge to human welfare as it would be in the research. Psychiatrist Robert N. Butler quotes Albert Einstein as having said that "with the atom everything changed except man's thinking." Apropos of this Dr. Butler notes, "Similarly, a cultural lag increasingly exists between medical progress and our understanding of its effects on the course of human life." [27] A special committee of representatives from twenty-six national health and welfare agencies recently endorsed the ecological viewpoint that medical care should be available to all who need it and not simply rationed among those who can afford it. Among those represented on the committee were the National Council of Aging, the American Federation of Labor, and the Congress of Industrial Organizations. The American Medical Association, speaking out of the other side of its mouth, was also on the list. In a statement declaring medical care to be a human right, the report asserted, "While determination of the amount and kind of medical care needed is a judgment of the health profession, the decision as to eligibility . . . should be a combined medical and social judgment." [28] It goes on to specify that to obtain medical services a family should not be cut off by some arbitrary income ceiling.

Private Initiative

The executives of Holiday Inns of America, the largest of all motel chains, are showing how modern business can perform an essential ecological service as soon as there is a commitment by society to health insurance programs. Within four days after Medicare became law, the chiefs of Holiday announced the formation of a new corporation—Medicenters of America. This single company will construct within a few years a national chain of 400 medicenters designed to fill the service gap between intensive hospital treatment and a return to normal life. Each medicenter will cost $1 to $2 million and will care for fifty or more patients at rates ranging from

$7.50 to $15.00 a day. Meanwhile regular hospital care now runs between $40 and $100 a day.

Theory

To return to our theory of the city—how does the evolution of new institutions appropriate to the needs of contemporary urban man relate to our concept of the city as a unique ecological system? If the well-being of the inhabitant is the function of the habitat—and if the function of society is the inclusion of the individual—then, as the environment changes, new accommodations must be made for all. The most significant of these changes are not those of physical form but of social organization—institutional evolution is the heart of environmental change. Institutional design is the *sine qua non* of urban design. A shell without content is a shell without life. The beauty of a city is a reflection of the beauty of its people—its ugliness is their ugliness. To apply cosmetics to the physical remains of a corpse does not restore the glow of life.

The herding instinct, which makes interacting social groupings desirable, guarantees that these groupings will persist and become more complex as families, tribes, ethnic groups, and races evolve into new associations appropriate to densely settled globally interrelated urban environments Only by becoming a part of these enlarged and more sophisticated associations can the individual, the family, the race, and nationality survive. In the modern synthetic environment employment, education, welfare, and medical care are highly institutionalized. It is the function of the society of responsibility to relate people fairly to one another through these institutions which are the means to food, shelter, and security in our times.

In his book, *On Aggression,* Konrad Lorenz has recorded in detail the rituals and organizational procedures which are employed by herding animals to restrain themselves from destroying one another through intra-specific aggression. Urban man faces a comparable problem. The question which any solution would have to respond to is how to construct a metropolitan environment of cities and suburbs that would tend to subordinate man's intra-specific aggressiveness to those herding instincts that make people effectively inter-dependent. In a synthetic habitat, where fallback upon natural resources is impossible, there can be no biologically successful existence for anyone who is not accepted into the herd which controls the technology of production and organization. General Motors, Ford, and Chrysler are performing not charity but a profoundly significant ecological function when they take the hard-core unemployed and make them operational. Beyond what private enterprise can do, the national society must do through government. Basic to the theory of the free-enterprise system is that it should operate at a profit. It cannot do this and accept responsibility for the social services that are a collective obligation of the whole nation and therefore an obligation of its government.

Perhaps we have emerged too recently from an agrarian society of rigidly structured human groupings which restrict and stratify to have learned how to regroup ourselves in flexible ways that allow for the widest social mobility. As long as the agrarian's individualistic code of proxemics dominates public policy there will be pronounced resistance to a universal, as distinct from a parochial-local, acceptance of mankind into society's biologically meaningful institutional network. A value system which ranks personal or privileged group indulgences above the essential needs of the generality is tolerable in an agrarian community in which even the poorest families may work the land for subsistence. As urbanization advances, and subsistence becomes dependent upon institutional affiliation, the agrarians' value system could become socially lethal were it to persist.

Just as the human embryo in its prenatal period of gestation passes through all the stages of organic evolution that preceded the emergence of man, so too does the citizen of a modern urbanized nation, if he is to thrive, pass through all the stages of social evolution on his way to social maturity. He is affiliated first of all with his family, clan, and tribe—then ultimately with those biologically meaningful institutions of national and international scope which train him to be functional within the broader society and which safeguard his health and security. A society of responsibility through its institutional networks is one that facilitates the full social maturation of all its citizens.

In a world that is becoming truly global in its resource technology, preparations for global security rather than global warfare are in order. The budgets of war could easily finance the institutions of a responsible society without additional taxation if the psychology of responsibility were gradually to displace the psychology of aggression. With just the $30 billion spent annually on the war in Vietnam, it would be possible to fund dramatic improvements in the institutions of peaceful coexistence. A 20 per cent improvement in all elementary and secondary schools could be achieved for an additional $5 billion annually. Present federal contributions to welfare services for the poor could be doubled for an additional $4.4 billion. The budgets for the notoriously bad mental hospitals run by states and localities could be doubled for an extra $1.2 billion. The buildings, equipment, and grounds of every college and university in the nation, both public and private, could be increased by 25 per cent for less than $6 billion.

Every public library in the nation could get a bonus of $100,000 for just $1.0 billion. Federal outlays for housing and community development could be doubled for an additional $0.6 billion. Federal expenditures for the recreational development and maintenance of national parks could be increased sixfold for $1.0 billion. For an extra $4.4 billion federal contributions to all road and highway construction could be doubled. Federal grants of assistance for educationally deprived children could be doubled for an additional $1.0 billion. Federal grants for school lunch and milk programs could be tripled for another $1.0 billion. All these improvements would amount to $25.6 billion, which would still be $4.4 billion short of the annual drain of the Vietnam war, the prosecution of which turned the once glowing prospects of a "Great Society" into bankrupt rhetoric and will do the same to President Nixon's "New Spirit" unless there is soon some new thinking at the highest levels where national priorities are defined.

Neanderthal man is believed to have existed for some 60,000 years, spanning perhaps 2,000 generations. He lived in a natural environment which he did not modify by either agriculture or any other technology. The average size of the adult Neanderthal's brain chamber seems to have been around 1,600 cubic centimeters compared with the average for modern man of about 1,450 cubic centimeters. From the study of Neanderthal graves some archeologists are of the opinion that he was a relatively peaceful creature and possibly became extinct when he got pushed around too much by the smaller but more aggressive humanoids who were our ancestors. Excavations of Neanderthal graves in Iraq's Shanidar cave have revealed that flowers were buried with the dead just as they are now. Possibly man's appreciation of beauty has changed very little since Neanderthal times. However, with the shrinkage of his brain something may have happened to that peaceful disposition, even though enough gray matter remained to create the wonders of modern science.

6

The Shell

———————————————

While the Apollo 8 spacecraft was orbiting the moon during
the last days of 1968 the Flat Earth Society of Great Britain
met in emergency session. "We have hardly had time to get
together to form an idea," remarked general secretary Samuel Shenton on December 24. Five days later, after viewing
TV photographs relayed from space, Shenton concluded,
"The Apollo pictures we saw on television merely showed
the earth as maps have shown it for several hundred years.
It was round in the sense of being circular but not in the
sense of being globe-shaped." He had declared earlier that,
if the pictures were not more convincing, "We shall continue fighting to prove the earth is flat." [1] No drop in membership was reported but it was a close call for the faithful.

The physical layouts of our cities suggest that the Flat
Earth Society is in charge. Urbanized land—the living and
working space for all but 5 per cent of Americans—is not
used to maximize the efficiency of industry and commerce.
Nor is it used to promote the convenience, safety, and beauty
of the environment. Land is not reserved as cities grow
wider and taller so as to have more space for circulation and
recreation. Quite to the contrary, the faster cities spread and
the denser populations become, the higher goes the price of
land so that less, rather than more, is set aside for circulation

and recreation. Land in cities, towns, and suburbs is managed to yield the highest profits to speculators and the highest
tax returns per acre to government. The approved and respected traditions of urban land management are precisely
the opposite of what is required to make the physical shells
of cities workable and livable. Members of the Flat Earth
Society are not alone in their ability to demonstrate the
power of positive thinking over positive evidence.

As long as land is treated as a commodity, the value of
which increases with population density, then just so long
will it be impossible to build cities that are efficient working
places and pleasant to live in. Mobility is a primary characteristic of urban existence. Resources are in constant motion
in and out of factories, warehouses, and distribution points.
As standards of living rise the resources required to sustain
them increase fabulously. Waste products alone amount to
several tons per capita per year. Unlike farmers, urban populations are highly mobile, in almost constant circulation.
For convenience and efficiency the land set aside for movement should increase with population density. Just the opposite occurs. The greater the demand for space, the harder
it is to get so that the tendency is to squeeze and pack rather
than to loosen up. An environmental *rigor mortis* sets in
precisely when flexibility is most needed. At the heart of
this contradiction between the way urban land is used and
the way it ought to be used is the agrarian notion that land
is property. It is totally at variance with the city's requirements.

People in the city are not farmers who depend upon land
to give them security, employment, and food. Urban populations depend upon their network of institutions to fulfill all
those basic needs. Because their prime ecological relationship
is not with land but with institutionalized society, land has a
subordinate, supportive role to play in the city in contrast to
its dominant role on the farm. A family's well-being in the
city is not measured in acres. The measure is dollars of in-

come. Land, then, should enhance the efficiency of the economy to raise per capita income. It should be used to accommodate all the activities that give quality to life as efficiently and economically as technology will allow.

Urban land should have no price and it should not be for sale if it is to be used effectively in that supporting role. It should be used as it is needed to give quality to life and to promote technological efficiency, precisely because the quality of life and the efficiency of the economy are directly dependent upon the way land is used. If cities are to have appropriate physical shells then a fundamentally new approach to land management will have to be devised. The present system, by which land becomes increasingly costly the more it is needed, results in congested, polluted, and ugly landscapes that are diametrically at odds with the purposes of the urban environment.

Leasing

The Irvine Ranch Company of southern California owns approximately 150 square miles of what might be called empty space on the southern edge of the Los Angeles metropolitan area. The company is engaged in an experiment in land management. If it is successful, and greedy local governments do not tax it into premature development, it may be able to come up with a new way to organize landscapes for the city of the future. Irvine is building three new towns. It has enough space to build a few more as time goes on and urbanization pushes south on its way to San Diego. What is distinctive about Irvine's operations is that the company has not sold or otherwise alienated its land except for a few relatively small parcels that accommodate an industrial park and a new campus for the University of California.

The greater part of the Irvine development is residential housing constructed by private contractors on spaces leased for seventy-five years. House lots are parts of larger tracts within each of which the leases expire simultaneously. The expiration dates of the tracts are staggered. If all goes well this means that about three-quarters of a century from now large blocs of land will again become available to the Irvine Company to do with them as it sees fit in terms of the needs and opportunities of the times. From then on, theoretically, 150 square miles of choice urban landscape—larger than Detroit—will be on a predetermined rotation schedule. Assuming that new modes of transportation will have replaced the means used today, and assuming that new, more efficient structures for industry and housing will have been invented, as well as new systems of community air conditioning, water supply, sewage treatment, waste disposal, and commodity distribution, then the landscape at Irvine can be painlessly redesigned to accommodate them. There will be no fuss about exercising rights of eminent domain or haggling over compensations to be paid to the owners of obsolete properties. Everything will be completely amortized including all community facilities: streets, sewers, water systems, and utility lines.

If there is one thing that is certain about the future it is the certainty of change. Massive investments by industry and the Federal Government in research and development—now running at the rate of $23.8 billion annually—cannot help but outmode nearly every aspect of life within the next seventy-five years, materially as well as psychically. The impact upon ways of life, goals, and values will be drastic. The physical shell will be forced to change accordingly. Landscapes will have to be flexible so as to adapt to change. Institutional change stimulated by the combination of technological innovation and direct participatory decision-making will accelerate. Possibly the Irvine Company picked up its idea of urban land rotation from its past experience with farm operations—planting wheat one year and clover the next. Now it is ranch houses today and who knows what seventy-five years from now.

What might be called the "Irvine Principle" is significant because it completely changes conventional concepts about how to manage urban land. Instead of being subdivided and sold to many small-lot owners at the highest possible prices it is offered to entire communities as a service—in a single, well-organized package. The company becomes, in effect, a public utility. What it provides is a service—land laid out in as efficient, convenient, and aesthetically pleasing manner as good planners can imagine and tailored to the purposes and technology of the times. The company holds a monopoly just as a telephone company, a water company, or a power company holds a monopoly. By holding a monopoly it is in a position to organize its service more efficiently than a collection of private speculators, each in competition with the others, could possibly do. Telephone companies do not sell telephones and then go out of business. They provide a continuing service at a fixed rate. Irvine provides land to whole communities on the same basis. Under such a scheme land ceases to be a commodity. It cannot be bought or sold. It becomes instead a function. Its job is to make the community work as well as possible by so spacing the pieces of its physical shell that congestion, pollution, and ugliness are avoided. This is a refreshingly urban way of looking at land —invented by an agricultural corporation.

The conventional practice in urban land management is totally different and largely responsible for the inability of communities to replace and rearrange their physical shells in response to technological changes and human desires. Present conditions have been brought about by the fact that urban land is bought and sold in thousands of little pieces to individuals and corporations with no prospect whatever that they might ever get together to organize the total landscape for the best interests of the community. Instead of sharing a common interest all have overpowering personal interests, some of which conflict. Speculation takes precedence over rational space allocation. This is not antisocial behavior or selfishness at all. It is playing the game according to the rules as they were set up in the agrarian past when land was the prime source of wealth. Because city revenues are tied to the property tax, city government, as a rule, goes along with almost any proposal to increase property values regardless of what happens to the community's total activity pattern. Because land values increase precisely as population density increases the resistances to rational space allocation multiply when it is most necessary. Functional land use design becomes an impossibility just as it becomes critically urgent—all planning boards, zoning boards, and League of Women Voters' watchdog committees to the contrary notwithstanding. This is why it is cheaper and easier in the long run to go off and build new suburbs or entire new towns rather than try to make the old urban cores either functional or livable.

The most effective way out of this bind is to take urban land off the market entirely. Land cannot possibly be used for the most efficient rearrangement of structures and activities as technology changes if its cost rises as a consequence of the population explosion. More land cannot be reclaimed for parks and playgrounds to service increasing populations if population increase itself skyrockets the price of land. The economics of land managed as property are diametrically at odds with the need for land to be managed as a service in the urban environment. Possibly what cities need are powerful investment combines which will buy up all urbanized and all urbanizable lands, consolidate them, and manage them as monopolistic public utilities according to the Irvine Principle.

Territoriality

A dispute has been going on for some time between schools of animal behaviorists and social biologists as to whether or not man has an innate territorial instinct. Does he, or does he not, have a primitive urge to possess a piece of ground that he can identify as his own and from which others are warned to stay away? Believers in territoriality claim it is a drive so overpowering that if it cannot be sublimated or re-directed by acculturation then accelerated urbanization to-gether with population increase will produce critical masses of humanity deprived of territorial roots and ready to ex-plode. If, however, territoriality is a manifestation of an even deeper instinctive need for security, then disaster may be averted if people attain security through status in their institutional networks rather than through land ownership. If security is the basic prerequisite for decent social behavior then "possession" of a piece of land would be less meaning-ful to the individual than if that land were used in the most effective way to give him privacy and to service those insti-tutions that give him status.

New Towns

There are seventy-five new towns in the United States, either in the process of construction or about to come off the draw-ing boards. Among their sponsors are Alcoa, Gulf Oil, Kaiser, Humble Oil, Penn Central Railroad, Goodyear, and Gen-eral Electric. Corporate giants are involved in new-town building because it gives them firsthand experience with an industry that just might balloon into the future's biggest growth operation. Present construction methods because of union-imposed building codes are among the most backward of contemporary technologies. A revolution in both architec-tural principles and land-assembly systems is long overdue. It will come as the big companies move into mass-produced cities and modern engineering displaces medieval craftsman-ship. Homebuyers may well decide that it is not worth the strain at 7½ to 8 per cent interest on FHA mortgages to go into debt for $30,000 or $40,000 on a house that will be obsolete before it is paid off.

Much cheaper, more efficient, better-equipped living spaces already are available where politically motivated building codes are not in effect. For the moment there is no closer alliance in most communities than that between local politics, the building-trade unions, materials suppliers, financiers, lawyers, home furnishers, and realtors. The higher the cost of a house the higher the tax base for local government and the bigger the rake-off for everyone else. In suburbia zoning laws that require half-acre to three-acre lots are used to force homebuyers to buy more land than they need to raise the tax base and to make it more difficult for poor people to become residents. The official explanation for these zoning regulations is that they prevent crowding. If that were the objective crowding could be avoided by an imaginative park, parkway, and playground system, but public open spaces do not produce revenue. The only one to get hurt by the present land use and housing formula is the little man who signs on the dotted line and agrees to foot the bill. There is hope for this little man if the mass production industries get into housing and land management the way they got into automobile transportation.

The movable house is already popular in the form of the mobile home or "trailer." Approximately one out of every nine new homes built in the United States is this type, which is ideally suited to factory methods and to the ever-shifting existence of the average family. To have a house on wheels means a saving of anywhere from 5 to 10 per cent on realtors' commissions, lawyers' fees, and bank paperwork every time the boss says, "The company needs you at the Peoria Division." But because of the property-tax basis of local government, trailers are already such a financial drag on some communities that they are outlawed. A $5,000 to $10,000 property evaluation on a mobile home is not enough at going assessment rates to pay the public service costs of an average family. Now the "disposable home" exists in trial form and could be mass-produced at low cost if local governments would permit. Of course, they will not permit as long as they have to get most of their revenues from taxes on residences. For the instant house a cheap slurry of polyester resins and chopped fibers is made into shells by high-speed injection molding. Prepackaged plumbing, heating, and wiring sets are available. Cornell University has issued a report, "The New Building Block," which lists ideas from around the world on how to build suitable shelters out of throw-away materials.

Engineers at Cornell foresee the time when home owners who want to renovate will simply unbolt unwanted rooms, send them to the dump, and replace them with something new out of a catalogue. New housing systems are made possible by inventions in synthetic materials that are not only cheap but lightweight. They have the added advantages of being strong, permacolored, waterproof, and efficiently insulated. They require little on-site labor, which is what the construction craft unions specialize in. Architect-engineer R. Buckminster Fuller, who designed the "skybreak" bubble which housed the U. S. exhibit at Montreal's Expo '67, has already worked out the mathematics of a lightweight tensegrity structure which could canopy an area two miles in diameter and almost a mile high at the center—enough to stretch across Manhattan Island from the Hudson to East River. With such a weather shelter the climate of an entire small city could be man-made. There would be no need at all for individual heating or air-conditioning units. All structures could be greatly simplified for none would have to resist either winds or weather. Fuller's basic thesis is that technological progress means an ever-increasing capability "to do more with less." New housing systems and total new-town plans call for more fresh thinking and less muscle-labor carpentry, masonry, and plumbing. New materials and new mass production technologies are ready for application.

The National Association of Home Builders Research Foundation, Inc., does not think that an all-new material or construction system will be discovered that could substantially cut housing costs. At least this is the opinion of staff vice president Ralph J. Johnson. The Association probably has not been looking very hard for anything startlingly new since it would mean the end of conventional practices and materials that make home building so profitable for everyone but the home owner. It would probably also mean the end of the Research Foundation. When former President Lyndon Johnson picked an eighteen-man Committee on Urban Housing it collected its data, of all places, from the present housing industry. Thus, it was no surprise when it reported back after more than a year of study that any revolutionary breakthrough in the technology of home building could be compared with "catching lightning in a bottle." It is not likely that government is going to find answers any faster than the National Association of Home Builders if it does not know where to look. Certainly the labor unions and materials suppliers who are locked into present systems of home building are not going to recommend changes that would open the doors to less time-consuming methods and cheaper components.

As ways of life change and as new technologies evolve at an ever-accelerating pace, there will be less inclination to invest in high-cost permanent structures that will soon be outmoded. Customer requirements eventually will force industrial change and if the small entrepreneur is too hidebound, imaginative big business will move in. The D. Overmyer Company, one of the largest truck terminal cargo transfer organizations in North America, expects its most recent depot structures to be obsolete in seven years because the technology of cargo handling is undergoing such rapid change. The disposable trucking depot is almost a must. Every existing office tower is fast going out of date as computerized systems of data storage, retrieval, and transmission make obsolete the honeycombed glass boxes designed for present office equipment and office routines. Standard school and university classrooms, as well as conventional instructional procedures, have been outmoded by the computerized library, TV and electronic fact-assembling and print-out devices. Only the reluctance of professors to become students again and of students to stretch and become their own instructors prevents new efficiencies and fresh excitements from being introduced into the university process which manages to question everything but itself.

Sunset International Petroleum Company of California is a builder of new towns. "I think we do it with a finesse and on a scale that deserves analysis," Sunset president Morton A. Sterling told a gathering of the Stanford Business School Alumni Association. "Our method has identified us not only as a developer of 'new towns' but also as a 'management builder.'" The largest of this company's four towns now under construction is, of course, Sunset—a place of twenty square miles, or a little larger in area than Albany, New York. It is eighteen miles north of Sacramento. During the next fifteen years it will be filled with 120,000 people. Sacramento itself had 191,000 inhabitants in 1960.

Sunset's operations are computer-programmed. This method schedules the flows of materials, labor, financing, and sales from start to finish. "Our concept is to manage the activities of hundreds of subcontractors," explains Mr. Sterling. "We combine their effort into a meaningful system that produces a total city or community from raw land. This means we create, plan, arrange, and supervise all aspects from the contracting of construction through the stage of finished building and the installation of water and sewer lines . . . We project a total community plan, which encompasses not only a careful balance of a variety of residential units and business and commercial facilities, but full provision for schools, churches, medical facilities, appropriate distribution of shopping areas, and last but not least, recreation facilities and country clubs." Land is used to support the efficient functioning of community institutions and laid out to avoid pollution, congestion, and ugliness. It is an urban, not an agrarian, approach to town building.

With the exception of the Irvine Ranch Company none of the big new-town builders operates on the leased-land principle. Therefore the time will come when they have sold their last lots and are ready to walk off and leave the place. From the community standpoint this is a weakness for there is no provision in that system for amortizing present structures both private and public by some predetermined date when life styles, housing tastes, and community layouts may be different and when the whole landscape could be done over accordingly. Also present new-town builders are using conventional building techniques and materials. They are operating on a larger scale and achieving certain economies because of that, but they are not yet far enough along to try Kleenex architecture or perpetual land management. Memorial park associations have long been willing to look after the future of those without a future but a land management service for ongoing communities of the living is largely an unexplored field. It might be a good one for insurance companies and pension funds. Both are accustomed to taking the long view.

Investment Capital

Pension funds, insurance companies, and other accumulators of mass capital now own 33 per cent of all publicly held stock. John C. Bogle, president of the Wellington Management Company, predicts that institutional ownership of such stock may rise to 40 per cent by the mid-1970's. He describes institutionalization of the security markets as "the growing share of equity ownership by financial institutions such as mutual funds, corporate pension funds, insurance companies and endowment funds." He sees this trend as an effective stabilizer of the economy. By taking the long view the big investment corporations tend to pass up fast-buck speculation to concentrate on enterprises that will grow steadily over time with the economy and technological progress. Cities might well be better off if these companies owned 40 per cent or even 100 per cent of all urbanized land and managed it in perpetuity as public utility monopolies according to the Irvine Principle.

Land under such public utility ownership would cease to be a commodity for speculators to play around with. Politicians would have less chance to arrange deals. Land under public utility ownership would be leased as a service at rates which could go up only if the community were to prosper because its landscape was attractive and efficiently organized. Present speculative land butchering tends to maximize the value of a few plots of ground to the detriment of others. This results in pollution, congestion, and ugliness. A single land manager would have to make the whole *system* serve effectively all the interests of the community. Just to remove temptation the monopoly licenses granted to such public utility land servicers should stipulate that they do not engage in any real-estate development of their own lest that conflict with the best interests of the total community.

Insurance companies, endowment funds, and pension funds have been in the real-estate business for a long time. They own some of the largest apartment developments in big cities. Connecticut General Insurance Company is the chief investor in Columbia, Maryland, the new city for one-quarter of a million people that is growing up between Baltimore and Washington, D. C. Since they operate on an actuarial basis they are accustomed to evaluate risks over time. Dealing with people and their life cycle they know that well-managed real estate for an increasing population with increasing longevity is one of the safest of all long-time investments. Few investments could be more secure than those that are hedged by population increase and urbanization. But, to make them even more attractive, communities could enter into long-term partnerships with land-holding public utilities backed by the authority of government and the abundant wealth of pension funds and insurance companies.

Nothing could so effectively guarantee the security of investments in land-management public utilities as a firm understanding with governments that the two would collaborate in their development commitments on the basis of continuous planning and budgeting. The private corporations could provide the investment funds to assemble land while government could agree to extend public facilities and public services only to those lands as they are developed according to design, and with time limitations on leases mutually agreed upon. Such an arrangement would be equivalent to the stipulations now accepted by all who purchase telephone service and electric power. The companies have monopoly franchises. In turn they accept government regulation. The usual returns of 7 to 9 per cent per year on capital, together with the safety factor, is enough to make them blue chips. If there were only one publicly regulated private land-management company in control of space allocation in a community it could prevent the chaos and ugliness that results from speculation. As long as urbanized land is available to countless speculators vying with each other for quick capital gains, orderly landscapes are a most unlikely result. Furthermore there is no provision for future land-use conversions on a wide-area basis under the fee-simple ownership system.

Provisions that will permit large-scale landscape erasures and conversions in the future are essential. In an urban environment, freedom of circulation is as important as the arrangement of accommodations and activities. Who can predict how long present motorcar and highway systems will remain practical? To what extent is the most efficient use of motor vehicles already handicapped by street and road patterns laid out for horse-drawn wagons? Every community that is more than seventy-five years old knows the reality of that problem, yet it goes on living with it because land uses frozen long ago are still legally valid. The present impact of the

truck, automobile, bus, airplane, and helicopter on architecture and landscape design could not have been anticipated
seventy-five years ago. What is being done now to adapt landscapes for the efficient use of hydrofoils, hovercraft, and air-
jet flying harnesses capable of flying electronic beam paths in
three-dimensional space? How soon will the latest super-
freeway be outmoded by electric vehicles with automatic
guidance systems using special rights-of-way? The present
systems of land use, which retard the introduction of technological innovations, were designed by land speculators,
most of whom are already dead or soon will be—yet communities must live with their shortsighted commitments
long after they have become obsolete.

A Sense of Change

Essential to good urban planning is a sense of both change
and continuity. The two are not in conflict. Corporations,
as contrasted with individuals, have an unlimited life ex-
pectancy. If they do their jobs properly, they anticipate
change and create change by responding to the need for
change. The better they respond, the better their chances
of continuity and the more powerful they become. Such a
sense of change and continuity is essential to environmental
design if the urban physical shell of landscapes and structures is to be flexible and continue to respond to new ways
of life and new technologies. The individual landowner and
land speculator does not have a long-range viewpoint because
his own life is too short. His impulses with respect to real
estate are inherently opportunistic. The quick profit while he
is alive is better than the steady dividend after he is dead.

A farmer in a static agrarian society had quite a different
attitude toward land. He was not a speculator. Since the
soil was the basis of his security, he held on to it. He did not
anticipate changes either in technology or in his way of life.
When the first settlers came to New England, they not only

cleared forests to create farms, but picked up and removed great quantities of heavy rocks from the surfaces of the fields. These they laid up into stone walls around pastures, plowland, and barnyards, along lanes, and around property bounds. To clear land and build walls were tasks that took the entire lifetimes of families. Today most of the fields in rural New England have reverted to woods but the stone walls still stand as a testament to the faith of those who first settled that their sons and heirs for generations to come would have land of their own and therefore security because change was not anticipated. But the industrial revolution made it easier to earn a living in the mill town than on the subsistence farm. The stone-walled fields were abandoned by those for whom they were intended.

The modern urbanite in the synthetic environment of constantly changing technologies, institutions, and landscapes is without the pioneer settler's illusion of permanence although he has just as strong a desire for security. He knows that whatever the most viable institutions of the moment may be, and whatever the arrangement of landscapes to accommodate them, all will change. For him, security is an adaptability to change. Land is no longer a treasure that grants protection to its owner. It has become a function which is to accommodate whatever institutions are viable at the moment and which in turn give him security through status.

Planners

As top political administrator of the world's most complex metropolitan area, New York's Governor Nelson Rockefeller is aware of the shortcomings of local zoning ordinances and the need for area-wide coordination of land uses in urbanized regions. "Planning used to be a word scorned by politicians. That is no longer true," the Governor told more than two-hundred urban planners at Conference 2020 called to make predictions about the urbanized landscapes of the next fifty years. A poll conducted at the conference by Elmo Roper indicated that 70 per cent of the experts dreamed of a web of concentrated central cities loosely woven together by a tissue of outlying but also concentrated "mini-city" nodes—all connected by new transportation systems. They declared themselves dissatisfied with what planner Boris S. Pushkarev described as the "spread city"—an amorphous scatteration of haphazardly dispersed suburban developments that consume space but leave little land for recreation or adequate transportation facilities.

The suburban "development" is the easiest route to profit for the small-scale real-estate speculator-salesman—and the most expensive and impractical for the public to service economically. Since these developments are uncoordinated promotions they eventually fill up the landscape by fusing with one another. They usually lack any particular locational advantages; so they are rural slums in the making. Their original attraction is open countryside, which continued development eventually eliminates. The next generation will want neither their quickly out-of-date houses nor their monotonous isolation. The hippie pads of great cities already are overpopulated with teen-age suburban refugees.

To introduce some rational design into this chaotic free-for-all, Governor Rockefeller advocates an increased coordination of long-range land-use and transportation planning among localities. He also recommends the wider use of Urban Development Corporations, which in New York State have the power to override the zoning restrictions of localities to achieve more rational and flexible landscape development. Neither politicians nor professional planners are ready as yet for such drastic instrumentalities as the monopoly-franchised public utility land-managing corporation that would operate on the leased-land principle. A few more decades of compounded congestion, pollution, and ugliness may bring them around to that decision about the year 2020.

Time Zoning

Most communities are familiar with zoning regulations which prescribe specific kinds of land uses. The theory behind use zoning is that some uses are compatible while others are not. Homes and schools go together. Airports and homes do not. By zoning the landscape of a metropolitan area, compatible uses are allowed to mix while the incompatible are segregated. The fallacy of zoning for use is that uses change with technological and cultural change. New uses develop, old ones expire, some uses expand while others shrink. It is impossible at one point in time to anticipate what the space needs of the future will be. This applies as much to private needs as to public needs. Frozen land-use patterns that conform to the past promote congestion, pollution, and ugliness. Zoning boards of appeal are established with legal power to grant variances. Under the pressures of change, incremental conversions accelerate; eventually the original zoning designs crumble. This is inevitable unless the zoning ordinances are rigidly adhered to. If adhered to rigidly while the way of life changes, the zoned landscape degenerates into a slum because it is disfunctional. Either way a problem develops.

In line with the concept that land in cities should be treated not as property but rather as though it had a service function to perform, I have previously proposed "Time Zoning" as a more suitable approach to space management than zoning for use. "Time Zoning" would help a community of many individual landowners accomplish some of the goals that a community with a single landowner might accomplish if the Irvine Principle were employed. Time zoning would fix precise dates in the future at which all owners of existing structures within a particular time zone would be expected to have amortized their investments in those structures. Thus they would be prepared to have old buildings demolished so that the total landscape of the zone could be simultaneously redesigned and allocated to whatever uses might then be appropriate for the next time period. The lengths of time periods for zones could be altered at the beginning of each lease period—shortened or extended as the changing character of the community might dictate. With its realistic emphasis upon the ephemeral rather than the illusory everlasting, time zoning would encourage shifts to an adaptive architecture. Structures of a particular cultural value such as monuments could of course be built and preserved as they are now without freezing whole landscapes.

Under time zoning owners of land would not lose their properties, but they would have to make them available for whatever uses might be suggested by changing technologies and ways of life. Owners would collect annual service charges but they would not be permitted to prescribe uses. They could not speculate but they would be guaranteed fair returns on their equities. Within the real-estate profession itself there is a distinction between the "salesmen" and the "investors." Time zoning would encourage the growth and responsibility of investment realty operators while it would discourage sales except to the investment realty corporations. As it is now the investment realtors, with their long-range concern for future as well as present values, are more aware of the pressures for change and they tend to work with them rather than against. Time zoning, too, may have to wait until the year 2020.

Arvida

Before he died, Arthur Vining Davis, former chairman of the Aluminum Company of America, organized the Arvida Corporation, an acronym of his own name. It is Arvida's plan to acquire 100,000 acres of land in a section of Florida which

extends from Delray Beach in Palm Beach County to Homestead, south of Miami in Dade County. It took Mr. Davis
twelve years to get titles and options to most of that property. When present objectives are realized Arvida will have
6,500 acres in Delray and Boca Raton in Palm Beach County,
including approximately a mile and a half of choice ocean
frontage. The company will have 23,000 acres of strategic
space in Broward County, west of Fort Lauderdale and
Hollywood. In Dade County it already holds 72,000 acres,
which is the largest block of privately held real estate in the
Miami area. It remains undeveloped for the most part but
it is suitable for residential and commercial sites. Were
Arvida to adopt the Irvine Principle and remain an investment realtor rather than become a salesman it could be
the principal trustee of rational land-use evolution in southern Florida—an area of unique beauty but unmercifully exploited by speculators. As a consequence of the frenetic in-
trigue that speculation generates, southern Florida between
West Palm Beach and Homestead easily could become the
southern counterpart of the New Jersey metropolitan slum
that extends from New York-Newark to Camden-Philadel-
phia. Consolidated land investors such as Arvida offer one
possible avenue of escape from congestion, pollution, and
ugliness if they can "get it together."

A new scale of land assembly and management is necessary
to cope with the new scale of population concentration that
modern urbanization creates. A characteristic of all expert
management is a capacity to respond to change by giving
rational guidance to change. An urban society must invent
new systems of space allocation which are flexible enough
and large enough in scale to work effectively with the future
rather than against it. Arthur V. Davis did not put all his
capital into Arvida. In addition he owned land in the Ba-
hamas and he held interests in nurseries, airlines, farms,
cargo ships, banks—and about a million shares in Alcoa. Obviously he must have seen some connection between institu-

tional evolution and the physical shell of contemporary urban society. Also he had more than a theoretical knowledge of how to collaborate with government.

When Mr. Davis died, the Penn Central Railroad bought 51 per cent of Arvida's stock. It is fully capable of carrying on in the business of relating land management to transportation and general development. Among its other assets Penn Central holds the controlling interest in the Macco Realty Company—a land management and development enterprise in southern California. It is a major stockholder in the Great Southwest Land Corporation of Arlington, Texas, which has produced one of the most remarkable commercial-industrial parks with boulevards, golf links, and formally landscaped grounds—more attractive than many new residential areas in suburbia. Its territory lies strategically between Dallas and Fort Worth, and one of its gems is The Greenhouse.

While fashionable ladies go to The Greenhouse to recover from urban tensions and to avoid decision-making, Penn Central itself thrives on both. It is busy building new cities and renewing the cores of old ones. And it knows how to link them together with transportation systems. It is presently collaborating with the Federal Government to develop high-speed rail service from Boston, through New York to Philadelphia, Baltimore, and Washington—the continuously urbanized area which French geographer Jean Gottmann called Megalopolis. Inspired by Gottmann's concept of an interstate city stretching from Boston to Washington, Senator Claiborne Pell of Rhode Island persuaded his colleagues in Congress to authorize Penn Central to develop in Megalopolis a more serviceable railroad spine. Penn Center, Philadelphia, the rejuvenated heart of one of America's slummiest urban deserts, is Penn Central Railroad's pride and joy—a twentieth-century commercial complex retrieved from a nineteenth-century rail yard, and made possible because one company owned the land, controlled its uses, and was willing to collaborate with local government to change old uses for new ones at the appropriate time.

The Growth of Physical Shells

At present the urbanized area of the United States is about 2 per cent of the national landscape. It seems likely that this percentage will increase dramatically by the year 2100 unless present landscapes become "erasable," and thus reorganizable, as populations grow and needs change. Agriculture cannot be counted on to thwart urban sprawl. In the first place, farmers are anxious to sell out to developers who will pay more for land in one lump sum than they could earn in a lifetime of hard work raising crops or livestock. Also, the trend in farm technology is to produce more and more food and fiber on less and less acreage with greater inputs of capital and inanimate energy. Fewer farms and less farm land will be needed in the future. Possibly by the year 2100, food production in factories powered by nuclear energy will have replaced field production dependent upon solar energy. Synthetic fibers are already with us—a major reason why it is so costly for the public to keep its inefficient cotton and wool producers in their obsolete occupations.

Without agriculture as a potential barrier to urban sprawl, cities will expand rapidly unless their most inefficient areas can be periodically reclaimed through time zoning or the wise management of land-holding public utilities. Present horizontal suburban dispersion, facilitated by highway networks and the private automobile, consumes over twice as much space per capita as the traditional central city. Just assuming the nation's population were to grow in the future at rates which have prevailed since 1900, there would be an eightfold increase by the year 2100. Assuming also that suburban sprawl continued to consume twice as much space per capita, then as much as 32 per cent of the United States could be urbanized by the year 2100. The formation of slums and other obsolete landscapes could be counted on to increase at least arithmetically if not geometrically. They would be somewhere between eight and sixty-four times as extensive as they are now. The resulting congestion, pollution, and ugliness would be unimaginable except to someone now living in Newark, New Jersey; Harlem; Oakland, California; South Chicago; or Gary, Indiana.

Considering how much inefficiency is already evident in the way urbanized land is utilized, it would seem that several things might happen in the intervening years between now and the year 2100. Population growth may slow down either voluntarily or by compulsion. Or there may be introduced new and far-reaching controls over the uses of urbanized spaces. Or a state of disorder could develop that would reduce the efficiency of new technologies and the overall productivity of the environmental system. The sharpening of social conflicts between classes and races which coincided with the Johnson Administration may be danger signals. They were, after all, the consequences of intensified urbanization without either private enterprise or government being willing to get together on an effective scale to reorganize customs, institutions, and landscapes.

Consequences

Obviously there is a potential for both environmental abuse as well as improvement in large-scale public utility monopoly management of urban real estate and transportation facilities. Such powerful centralized control could result in callous arrangements indifferent to human sensitivity and guided strictly by a profit motive. Even so, profit motives differ. The fast-turnover speculator has a different concept of profit from that of a long-term investment realtor. It is a question of which type is likely to produce the better ecological result. To be realistic, it is obvious that centralized control over the allocations of space and the development of transportation networks becomes increasingly essential as populations concentrate in urbanized areas and as institutions diversify, specialize, and grow in response to technological change. A healthy increase in direct participatory democracy might lead to more perceptive government regulation of land investment and management companies.

In the past the American public, through its city, state, and Federal governments, has proved to be incompetent as a rational designer and developer of its physical environment. Localities which have the chief political responsibility have the least political muscle and the weakest financial capabilities. The Federal Government, which has the most powerful regulatory authority with the fattest purse, has the least sense of commitment and will continue that way as long as Congressmen with the greatest seniority who head the most powerful committees continue to think with agrarian minds. Washington, through the under-financed urban-oriented executive agencies, says in effect to localities, "Get in there and fight while I hold your coats." Not only does it hold their coats but it picks their pockets while they get knocked out.

State governments, split by the conflicting interests of farmers, small towners, suburbanites, and urbanites, could do more. They have authority that transcends the petty geographic jurisdictions of localities, which is essential in an age of private institutions that intersect across the limited frontiers of local political fiefdoms. But state governments are almost as hard up as localities. Their pockets, too, are picked by the Federal Government, which soothes their representatives with pork barrel rivers, harbors, irrigation, and military post construction contracts, but which skittishly avoids the real problems of environmental management that have sunk localities and states deep in debt without having achieved real solutions to their problems. Those solutions are beyond the financial means of states and, in part, beyond their jurisdictional control as when a metropolitan region such as New York's spreads into two other states. To give proper government support to the complex institutional developments of urbanization and to exert the proper control over landscape organization that is needed to support the institutional networks, it may be necessary for both state and local governments to give way in favor of new regional governments with flexible geographic boundaries.

Under present circumstances, private enterprise, which is free to operate interstate, does well even to attempt to coordinate environmental development—and only the most powerful combines of financial and business interests could hope to introduce rationality where governments have failed. If there are those who might complain that this gives private enterprise too much leverage in the management of the public enterprise, it should be remembered that public enterprise has defaulted by putting the most responsibility on local governments which have the least muscle. As long as localities, which can do the least, are responsible for doing the most, the urban shell, together with all its public service institutions, will continue to degenerate. As economist Wilbur Thompson says, "To grow is to get bigger"—that is the problem. The faster the economy heats up, the richer Washington becomes, but the more services and physical facilities localities must provide to accommodate that growth. The further they sink into debt, the worse their services become. Prosperity drives local governments to the wall.

The increased responsibility for institutional development and for physical facilities that localities must bear with growing urbanization is too much for the agrarian property tax and too much for the limited talents and limited jurisdictions of local government. In an age of globalized private industry, financed by international investment pools, it is ludicrous for public industry to be financed by local property taxes. It is ecologically meaningless to have a vote for representative governments, local, state, and Federal, that are not structured to respond to the needs of the voter. The average voter hardly needed a war in Vietnam as a top priority item, but that is what he got rather than a comprehensive social-security system or a physical landscape with minimal pollution, congestion, and ugliness. He has least influence at the national level where the public money is and the most influence at the local level where it is not; the result of a complete reversal of priorities.

Rich Uncle

The little state of Rhode Island has fewer than one million people but they are densely packed—812 to the square mile. This exceeds the population densities of Japan, China, and India. The state's physical shell is antiquated. The cities are old—among the first settled in America. Some of its factories date back to the days of the industrial revolution. It is a place where it is unnecessary to buy antiques for atmosphere. A few years ago, the U. S. Army Corps of Engineers looked at the state's landscape and decided that it needed a hurricane barrier in Narragansett Bay. Citizen critics declared that a hurricane barrier would reduce tidal flushing and intensify the pollution of fishing grounds and resort beaches. Anyway, the Engineers decided to make plans and estimates. For $90 million, plus a maintenance fund of $11 million, the Corps in 1965 proposed to build the hurricane barrier and only charge the state $37.9 million for its share. Washington, it said, would pay $63.1 million. The Pentagon could afford to think big. Its own budget exceeds the total of all the budgets of all fifty states. The Corps of Engineers alone spends four times as much annually as the State of Rhode Island.

The people of Little Rhody panicked and rejected the proposal. The Engineers' bill for $101 million amounted to almost one-third of the total indebtedness of the state and all of its towns, school districts, and other public authorities. For what the Federal Government would have sunk into a superfluous hurricane barrier, the state and its towns could have bought necessary schools, roads, hospitals, fire stations, reservoirs, sewage plants, and the recreation areas they have long done without because they could not afford them. They could not get the Corps of Engineers to help them with these essentials.

Technology

Present urban shells are built as if the technology of earth-moving, rock-boring, and escalator-elevator lifts had not improved in the last fifty years. New earth-moving machinery developed for high-speed open-pit coal mining operations can literally create new topographies at minimal costs. Equally sensational are the latest high-speed earth-boring drills developed to cut tunnels through mountains for large-scale irrigation projects. New irrigation projects in New Mexico sponsored by the U. S. Bureau of Reclamation use rock-boring machines that dig tunnels thirteen to twenty feet in diameter at rates up to one hundred feet per day. If the mayors of America had as much influence in Congress as desert farmers producing surplus crops with publicly subsidized irrigation water, they would drag the Bureau of Reclamation into every major city that needs a subway system and put its contractors and their big machines to work drilling tunnels where the problem is a scarcity of clean, efficient mass transit facilities rather than an excess of crops that are dumped abroad.

In 1964, the Bucyrus-Erie Company of South Milwaukee delivered to the Peabody Coal Company a new electric power shovel which is used at its River King mine about thirty miles east of St. Louis. The shovel removes earth overburden to expose veins of coal that lie beneath. Weighing 18.5 million pounds, the shovel is the largest self-propelled land machine in the world. It digs 250 tons of earth at a single bite and moves twice as much ground as all seventy-seven of the power shovels which dug the Panama Canal. The beam of the Bucyrus-Erie shovel is as tall as a twenty-story building and it consumes enough electricity to supply a city of 15,000 people. This giant is manipulated by a single operator who is comfortably situated in an air-conditioned cab. Anyone visiting a modern strip mine, or even passing over one in an airplane, can easily imagine what this new generation of earth-moving machinery could do to reshape the topographies of cities if it were put to that work. The engineering equipment exists to make landscapes of any form or slope to suit any type of structure. What is lacking is the social and political equivalent of modern engineering techniques.

3-D

High-speed rail and mass transit systems running deep underground in tubes cut by rock-boring machines could be connected to the surface by escalators and elevators also running in tubes. Underground transportation vehicles, like aircraft, can operate in three-dimensional space which is impossible for surface vehicles operating on a plane. It is a simple matter of applying space-age geometry to the earth itself. Considering technological advances already achieved, mass transportation of people and materials could be accomplished in cities far more efficiently underground than on the surface if only the design and development of structures and activities at the surface were coordinated with the locations of the subways. Again it is a question of politics catching up with engineering.

The most singular advantages of underground tubes over surface transportation routes is that they would not intersect and crisscross on the same plane, causing congestion, delays, and hazards. Also the earth itself constitutes a ready-made structural support for the tubes. *Engineering News-Record* has reported on a proposal for high-speed tube trains as designed by Lawrence K. Edwards. Capsule cars gliding on steel rails could be pushed by air pressure and pulled by gravity through steel-lined tubes drilled through rock more than a half-mile below ground level. Speeds up to 400 miles per hour would permit travel from Boston to Washington in two hours with fifteen stops along the way. The whole trip could be made in less time than it takes a jet aircraft to come down out of a foggy night stack-up over Kennedy Airport. Surface trains now take more than eight hours.

That the underground should be so neglected while the surface becomes so cluttered with crisscrossing roads, tracks, and cables would be unexplainable if it were not for the fact that the layout of an efficient transportation-communication network must be coordinated with origins and destinations of traffic. Without control over the allocations of surface space it is impossible to locate underground routes economically. On the surface it is possible to improvise as numberless landowners make their separate decisions. From time to time, as appropriations are made piecemeal, it is possible to remove "bottlenecks" by highway surgery. Surface roads may be built by slow increments, going any way the action develops when budgets permit. To build sensibly in three-dimensional underground space requires from the beginning a concept of the completed system backed up by firm commitments to future surface space allocations. Considering the chopped-up patterns of private land ownership and the irrational overlapping of political jurisdictions it would be harder to organize the surface spaces than to construct the tubes below. Physical engineering is easy compared with human engineering.

Policy

Effective public policy with respect to the synthetic environment will be delayed for some time. Needed first of all is a drastic change in citizen thinking. The agrarian mind with all its eccentric values is incapable of inventing an appropriate environment for mass populations, which are dependent upon a synthetic resource technology. Neither an adequate physical shell nor the more important institutions of a genuine society of responsibility will evolve from a way of thinking that is convinced that scarcity is inevitable and that property, rather than talent, is the basis of security.

The agrarian mind is incapable of managing the technological potential for abundance. Its attitudes run contrary to the demonstrated capacities of industrial management to increase resource output per capita even while populations are increasing. Agrarian attitudes toward land, taxation, public utility monopolies, national sovereignty, and big government responsibilities were quite appropriate for an age of small family farmers circumscribed by the limits of nature. They are out of phase with the potentialities of the Einsteinian equation and its promise of inexhaustible energy translatable into resources. The capacities of intelligence to build upon intelligence is exemplified in the research-development industry, which is finding it possible to do ever more with less.

The agrarian mind has perverted this system to military suppression rather than creative ends because it is afraid of scarcity rather than confident of abundance. At the very moment in its cultural evolution, when for the first time it is possible to provide everyone with all-risk comprehensive insurance at birth, the nation, still operating like a society of farmers, calls for more police repression at home and more military commitments abroad. Psychological fixations carried over from the pre-nuclear age of limitations prevents fresh policy formulations appropriate for an urban age.

"Since the date of our earliest surviving records of human affairs, there has been a widening gap between mankind's ever-increasing technological prowess and the obstinate moral inadequacy of our social performance." This is the way Arnold Toynbee, from the perspective of history, reviews mankind's ability to master the natural world through the application of intellect and its failure to master itself.

New scales of productivity have come into existence within the past two decades, thanks to the vigor of the private economy and the evolution of mass production technologies. Now an accelerated globalization of the econo-technic network shows how those systems of mass-scale resource production could be brought to the underdeveloped world. But there are powerful socio-political resistances to such a liberation of the poor from want. The "moral inadequacy" is articulate and well armed. It is opposed to significant reform.

The agrarian-minded élites of underdeveloped countries use the political powers of national sovereignty to valve down the rate of investment by international corporations to proportions that they can control, either personally or in the names of their governments which they, in turn, command. The threat of confiscation in the name of national sovereignty is an effective lever used to preserve privileges for the élite at the expense of industrial expansion that would give others a chance to rise, socially and economically. It is the same mentality which prevents, although by different means, progressive industrial interests from opening up employment to Negroes beyond tokenism in the textile mills of South Carolina.

The masses of citizens within underdeveloped countries are, like the rural Negroes of the Deep South, uneducated, without marketable skills, and vioceless in political affairs. Having effectively deprived their own people of representation in government the élites resist the development of urban institutions within which participatory democracy could give common citizens a voice. The agrarian feudal system is authoritarian. The rationale behind it is that might makes right since there is not enough for everyone. Faced with the opportunities of an urban age of advanced industrial technology, such a society, by the employment of national sovereignty, prevents change in order to preserve its ancient privileges. Under the circumstances, private investment accelerates even faster in the already urbanized nations where the environment for an expanded economy is more favorable. The gap widens between the poor nations and the rich, but it does not cramp *La Dolce Vita* of the international jet set's beautiful people, whose private spending is not constrained by national sovereignty.

There is a genuine community of interest between the military establishments of developed nations and the feudal élites of underdeveloped countries. It is based upon their common agrarian concepts of the world habitat that overrides ideological differences whether they be Communist or capitalist. That mutual outlook stems from a conviction that security is to be measured in terms of territory controlled rather than in terms of economic development. National sovereignty takes precedence over the development of a rational international econo-technic network of resource-making, people-serving institutions.

The alliance between foreign militarists and the feudal élites inflates the nuisance value of national sovereignty, making it more difficult for foreign civilian investors in international productive economic enterprise to negotiate without submitting to extortion. Thus our own publicly financed foreign military aid tends to work against our own publicly subsidized civilian economic aid. They cancel each other out while the American taxpayer is dismayed at the lack of progress. Impoverished populations abroad become more desperate and rebellious. This, in turn, persuades the great rival powers to escalate their military aid. The wealth that might have been spent on economic development is spent upon repression with the same logic that produced the confrontations in Prague and Chicago.

In February, 1969, leading bankers and industrialists of the Western world met in Amsterdam to discover, if they could, what is holding back private investments in underdeveloped countries and to propose remedies. A study by Dirk U. Stikker, former Secretary General of the North Atlantic Treaty Organization (NATO), predicted that by 1975 virtually all foreign money going to underdeveloped countries will be required to pay back their installment payments and interest charges on previous investments. There will be no surplus left out of this exchange to build up additional productive plants. Dr. Stikker's analysis shows that unless foreign capital inputs are greatly increased after 1975, there will be a net drain of money out of the underdeveloped countries while their populations continue to increase.

Before he retired in 1969, the former Secretary General of the United Nations Conference on Trade and Development, Dr. Raul Prebisch, warned of "a great upheaval" in the underdeveloped world unless both developed and underdeveloped nations find new ways to utilize modern technology for their common good. He foresees "frustrated people" in Latin America, Africa, and Asia creating violent changes if evolutionary progress is not accelerated. Dr. Prebisch believes that agricultural technology can create trouble by its very success unless the surplus populations that are displaced by modern farm techniques are absorbed into urban industries. These industries cannot be created without capital. To build a synthetic environment that could utilize the incredible potential for abundance which is implicit in modern technology will require a revision of traditional economic and social structures. America must learn to make these changes at home, where obviously the chances of success are better than they are in the underdeveloped world, if it is to help avert the great upheaval of frustrated people which Dr. Prebisch and other thoughtful persons see in the offing.

America made land available to the landless in the nineteenth century when that was the proper answer to insecurity. Its job in the twentieth is to make status available within the institutional networks of the synthetic environment. It must discover how to do this not only because it is imperative at home, but because the synthetic environment of the city is the only hope for the mass populations of underdeveloped agrarian nations. Space itself no longer has ecological value

except as it is consciously developed to produce the inanimate energy and the resources that unconscious nature, manipulated by human muscles, cannot provide.

National sovereignty is meaningless to people who are
hungry except that it prevents them from crossing borders
into better organized states. National sovereignty does not
prevent their élites from depositing scarce surplus wealth in
anonymous accounts in Swiss banks. Deposed Latin American dictators or Middle East oil sheiks have no difficulty
living high on their transferred wealth at Miami Beach or
on the French Riviera. More meaningful than national sovereignty is the rate at which technological development through
rational international urbanization creates the institutional
networks that will give people everywhere employment and
status.

If international wars are to be averted, the synthetic environment with its people-relating institutions must be
strengthened. It is the only way to create abundance artifi-
cially through technology in a world of natural poverty. As
the well-being of all men everywhere is seen to be directly
related to the synthetic environment they have created, the
less likely are they to fall victim to any ideological persua-
sion. These measures of thought control were generated in
an age of scarcity to persuade the desperate but naive that a
change in political systems could result in economic abundance. Politicians promise happiness on earth as flippantly as
priests promise it in the hereafter. Such promises are beside
the point to those who realize that affluence is a quantity
fixed by the limits of technology. The world's capacity for
abundance is real. That is the message of modern science
which politicians the world over have not yet understood.

To create material abundance and a functional physical
environment requires that intelligence be able to produce
synthetically what does not exist naturally. This requires a
constantly increased investment in education and productive
plant. As intelligence develops and productive plant becomes

more conspicuous in all parts of the world, it will gradually be realized that any kind of social conflict, either locally or internationally, that might destroy the resource-generating synthetic environment would automatically put people in jeopardy. International peace and domestic tranquility would be sought with the same sense of self-preservation that now persuades people that civil strife and foreign wars are the solutions to their troubles. The politician will be downgraded in the process but what he loses will be recouped by people representing themselves by direct participatory action within their immediate institutional matrices.

There can be no security for any nation or for humanity as a whole as long as territorial control is given priority over investments in the technological means of resource production. The world is already so dependent upon these manmade sources of resources that any serious contemplation of nuclear war would be contemplation of global suicide. Not one person would have to be killed outright by modern war to destroy the human race. The destruction of existing capital investments would do it, for it is our man-made productive capability upon which all of us now rely for survival.

Any sensible policy for the American city begins with a general concept of the total world environment as it now exists. What is needed to take the edge off those bitter social conflicts which have surfaced in our cities at home is needed equally to ease the conflicts between the desperately poor two-thirds of the world and the one-third which now is sufficiently urbanized to generate its own resources. Political doctrine never created a kilowatt of energy or converted a molecule of atmospheric nitrogen into life-giving fertilizer. What is needed is no further subscription to political faiths but heavier investment worldwide in the technologies of production and a drastic cutback in the military technologies of waste.

The American ghetto will not cease to fester until its people are made viable members of a society of responsibility.

This cannot happen until localities are abundantly assisted by the wealth of the Federal Government transferred from the Pentagon to those civilian agencies and bureaus that are concerned with services to people and the construction of functional urban shells. To do their jobs properly, localities and states must receive massive financial help from the Federal Government through its executive departments.

By the same token, the underdeveloped world will experience continuous outbreaks of rebellions, civil wars, and international conflicts until its desperate and frustrated peoples have something to make peace worth keeping. The ragged Arab masses of the Middle East, who are without urban industries to employ them, will continue to vent their frustrations by sabotaging Israel, which, as a society of responsibility, has built cities for its own people. The wealth wasted on the Vietnamese war by all concerned could have built cities with power stations and industries that might have employed all the landless peasants of all Southeast Asia, and so removed the causes of their desperation. The globalization of industry now going on could be accelerated manyfold with the investment funds that would be available if the world were to urbanize for peace rather than arm for the preservation of outmoded agrarian societies.

The need to accelerate this globalization is obvious. World Bank President Robert McNamara, addressing his organization's annual meeting in 1968, revealed that "the annual growth of per capita income in Latin America is less than 2 per cent, in East Asia only about 2 per cent, in Africa only 1 per cent, and in South Asia only about half a per cent. At these rates, a doubling of per capita income in East Asia would take nearly thirty-five years, in Latin America more than forty years, in Africa almost seventy years, and in South Asia nearly a century and a half." [2] Since the annual per capita income in South Asia is now in the neighborhood of $70, it could, at present rates of income, become $140 by the year

2118. The average per capita income in the United States *increases* by at least $250 per year.

Surely when Governor Nelson Rockefeller made the rounds of Latin America for President Nixon in the spring and summer of 1969, he must have learned that accelerated urbanization backed by massive capital investments in modern technology is an immediate necessity in our hemisphere. Revived nineteenth-century talk about land reform is an anachronistic nonsensical diversion at a time when the land, no matter how it is divided, can no longer provide either the necessary resources or the necessary employment for the new mass populations already in existence. Worldwide, that is now the job of the city—that is what urbanization is all about. Sheer biological pressure creates the pressure for political and social change. The urge to make cities accommodate the human overflow is nothing less than the urge to stay alive. If those who hold the power of decision do not respond imaginatively to this elemental urge to exist violence will intensify. The masses of unskilled and ignorant have no capacity to formulate solutions. However, they do have a powerful biological urge to destroy whatever is unresponsive to their instinct to survive. The choice is between an imaginative, deliberately created urbanization that fully employs the wonder of modern technology for the ecological welfare of total world humanity, or universal genocide. Otherwise the very will to live will destroy life.

What are the probabilities of peace in a world where the populations of poor rural nations grow at twice the rate of those in rich urban nations while disparities in resources widen at present rates? That is the reality of our times and only a mammoth transfer of wealth from war to peace has any prospect of altering the collision course the whole world is set upon. If America is to operate on the larger scale of the world emergency—and there is very little lead time left— the best place to learn the strategy and methods is at home by solving quickly the problems of the poor and the black.

Police squads employing helicopters, mace, and armored cars or a war machine capable of the massacre at Song My are hardly such answers as the world expects of a nation that can send Apollo spaceships to the moon and create a gross national product that will exceed $1 trillion by 1972.

APPENDIX

Sources of Quoted Material

CHAPTER 1. THE TECHNOLOGICAL POTENTIAL

1. Fuller, R. Buckminster, *Nine Chains to the Moon*. Southern Illinois University Press, Carbondale and Edwardsville, 1967. P. 62.
2. Turner, Frederick J., *The Mississippi Valley Historical Review*, Vol. XXVII, No. 1, June 1940. P. 43.
3. Schlesinger, Arthur M., *The Mississippi Valley Historical Review*, Vol. XXVII, No. 1, June 1940. P. 52.
4. Piel, Gerard, *The Acceleration of History*. Reprint of Phillips Academy Address, April 27, 1963. Pp. 10, 21.
5. Adams, Henry, *The Education of Henry Adams*. Houghton Mifflin Company, Boston and New York, 1961. Pp. 491, 495–497.
6. Toynbee, Arnold J., *A Study of History*. Abridged by D. C. Somervell. Oxford University Press, New York and London, 1947. P. 211.
7. Schlesinger, Arthur M., *The Mississippi Valley Historical Review*, Vol. XXVII, No. 1, June 1940. P. 46.
8. *Congressional Record*. Washington, D.C., March 10, 1969. P. E1784.
9. *New England Council Action Report,* July 1968.
10. *The New York Times,* July 14, 1968.
11. *Saturday Evening Post,* 1968.

12. *Saturday Review,* November 23, 1968. P. 39.
13. *Congressional Record.* Washington, D.C., June 21, 1968. P. E5721.

CHAPTER 2. SOCIAL RESISTANCES

1. *The New York Times,* March 24, 1968.
2. *Ibid.,* March 16, 1969.
3. *Psychology Today,* August 1968. P. 18.
4. Horn, Francis H., *Honors Colloquium Address,* University of Rhode Island, December 2, 1968.
5. *Psychology Today,* August 1968. P. 66.
6. *Report of the National Advisory Commission on Civil Disorders.* Bantam Books, Inc., New York, 1968. P. 407.
7. *Ibid.,* pp. 390–392.
8. *Statistical Abstract of the United States, 1968.* U.S. Government Printing Office, Washington, D.C. P. 18. *The New York Times,* August 18, 1968.
9. *Report of the National Advisory Commission on Civil Disorders.* Bantam Books, Inc., New York, 1968. Pp. 390–392.
10. *The New York Times,* February 16, 1968.
11. *Providence Evening Bulletin,* July 18, 1968.
12. *The New York Times,* April 15, 1968. *Ibid.,* May 18, 1969.
13. *The Nation,* March 4, 1968. Pp. 306–307.
14. *The New York Times,* December 8, 1968.
15. *Ibid.,* April 12, 1969.
16. *Ibid.,* January 7, 1969.
17. *Chicago Tribune,* editorial, June 29, 1968.
18. *Statistical Abstract of the United States, 1968.* P. 596.
19. *Congressional Record.* Washington, D.C., October 13, 1966. P. 25625.
20. *Ibid.,* April 16, 1969. P. E2995.
21. *The New York Times,* February 16, 1969.
22. *Ibid.,* February 28, 1969.
23. *Ibid.,* May 3, 1969.
24. *Saturday Review,* December 14, 1968. P. 18.

CHAPTER 3. TOWARD A THEORY OF THE CITY

1. *The New York Times,* December 15, 1968.
2. *Ibid.*
3. Haggard, Ernest A., "Psychological Causes and Results of Stress," in *Human Factors in Undersea Warfare.* National Research Council, Washington, D.C. Pp. 441, 455.

4. Rennie, Thomas A. C., *Mental Health in the Metropolis*. McGraw-Hill Book Company, Inc., New York, 1962. Pp. 138, 230.

5. Calhoun, John B., "A 'Behavioral Sink,'" in *Roots of Behavior*, edited by Eugene L. Bliss. Harper and Bros., New York, 1962. Pp. 295–315.

6. *The New York Times*, May 18, 1969.

7. Lorenz, Konrad, *On Aggression*. Harcourt, Brace & World, Inc., New York, 1966. P. 258.

8. *Ibid.*, pp. 261, 263.

9. *The New York Times*, May 18, 1969.

10. *Ibid.*, April 20, 1969.

11. *Ibid.*, May 18, 1969.

12. Coulanges, Fustel de, *The Ancient City*. Lee and Shepard, Boston, 1889. Pp. 29, 177.

13. *Congressional Record*. Washington, D.C., December 4, 1967. P. S17766.

14. *The New York Times*, August 4, 1968.

CHAPTER 4. GOVERNMENTS AND BUDGETS

1. *Statistical Abstract of the United States, 1968*. U.S. Government Printing Office, Washington, D.C. P. 406.

2. *Ibid.*, pp. 378, 409.

3. *The Budget of the United States Government*. U.S. Government Printing Office, Washington, D.C. Fiscal Year 1970, p. 16; Fiscal Year 1969, p. 488.

4. *Facts and Figures on Government Finance—1969*. Tax Foundation, Inc., New York. P. 19.

5. *Ibid.*, p. 16.

6. *Statistical Abstract of the United States, 1968*. U.S. Government Printing Office, Washington, D.C. P. 479. Also, *The Budget of the United States Government*. U.S. Government Printing Office, Washington, D.C. Fiscal Year 1969. P. 544.

7. *Historical Statistics of the United States 1789–1945*. U.S. Government Printing Office, Washington, D.C. Pp. 295, 314.

8. *The Mayor and Federal Aid*. United States Conference of Mayors, Washington, D.C., 1968. Pp. 9, 73.

9. *The New York Times*, December 17, 1968.

10. *Congressional Record*. Washington, D.C., April 17, 1969. Pp. H2787–H2789.

11. *Ibid.*, March 22, 1965. P. 5443.

12. *The New York Times*, October 26, 1963.

13. *The Budget of the United States Government—1970*, pp. 16, 73, 406, 414. Also, *The Budget of the United States Government—1969*. U.S. Government Printing Office, Washington, D.C. P. 488.

14. *Farm Journal*, editorial by Wheeler McMillen. Also, *The New York Times*, February 16, 1969.

15. *Statistical Abstract of the United States, 1968*. U.S. Government Printing Office, Washington, D.C. P. 409.

16. *Facts and Figures on Government Finance—1969*. Tax Foundation, Inc., New York. P. 19.

17. *The New York Times*, September 22, 1968.

18. *Congressional Record*. Washington, D.C., October 2, 1968. P. E8493–E8494.

19. *Business Review*. Federal Reserve Bank of Philadelphia, June 1968. Pp. 16–17.

20. *Congressional Record*. Washington, D.C., December 15, 1967. Pp. S19054–S19055.

21. *The New York Times Magazine*, December 22, 1968.

22. *Ibid.*

23. *Statistical Abstract of the United States, 1968*. U.S. Government Printing Office, Washington, D.C. P. 120.

24. *Business Review*. Federal Reserve Bank of Philadelphia, April 1964. Pp. 13–18.

25. *Congressional Record*. Washington, D.C., December 11, 1967. P. A6086.

26. *Ibid.*, p. A6086.

27. *The New York Times*, March 23, 1969.

28. *Congressional Record*. Washington, D.C., March 10, 1969. Pp. S2518–S2523.

29. *Ibid.*, pp. S2518–S2523.

CHAPTER 5. A SOCIETY OF RESPONSIBILITY

1. *Saturday Review*, January 11, 1969. P. 52.

2. *Congressional Record*. Washington, D.C., December 8, 1967. P. S18245.

3. *Ibid.*, October 9, 1968. P. E8853.

4. *Ibid.*, October 28, 1968. P. E9448.

5. *Ibid.*, October 14, 1968. P. S12892.

6. *Ibid.*, October 28, 1968. P. E9448.

7. *The New York Times*, January 4, 1969.

8. *The Nation*, August 26, 1968. P. 136.

9. *U.S. News & World Report*, September 20, 1965.

10. *Congressional Record.* Washington, D.C., December 8, 1967. P. S18227.

11. *Ibid.,* August 15, 1968. P. E7509; June 30, 1968, p. E7120; November 7, 1967, p. H14805.

12. *Statistical Abstract of the United States, 1968.* U.S. Government Printing Office, Washington, D.C. Pp. 325, 479.

13. *Ibid.,* pp. 235, 465.

14. *Ibid.,* p. 276.

15. *Ibid.,* pp. 314, 315, 323.

16. *Ibid.,* p. 323

17. *Congressional Record.* Washington, D.C., August 11, 1969. P. H7244.

18. *Ibid.* Pp. H7239-41.

19. *The New York Times,* August 15, 1969.

20. *Congressional Record,* Washington, D.C., July 26, 1968. P. E7000.

21. *Ibid.,* August 2, 1968. P. E7310.

22. *The New York Times,* April 26, 1966.

23. *Ibid.,* June 28, 1969.

24. *Congressional Record.* Washington, D.C., July 26, 1968. P. S9453.

25. *Statistical Abstract of the United States, 1968.* U.S. Government Printing Office, Washington, D.C. P. 264.

26. Anderson, Oden W., Patricia Collette, and Jacob J. Feldman, *Changes in Family Medical Care Expenditures and Voluntary Health Insurance—A 5-Year Resurvey.* Harvard University Press, Cambridge, Mass., 1963. Also, Anderson, Roland, and Oden W. Anderson, *Progress in Health Services,* Vol. 14, No. 5, 1965, and Vol. 15, No. 1, 1966. Reports of Health Information Foundation.

27. Butler, Robert N., *Increased Longevity: Present and Future Challenge.* Mimeographed April 22, 1969.

28. *The New York Times,* June 28, 1964.

CHAPTER 6. THE SHELL

1. *The New York Times,* December 31, 1968.

2. *Congressional Record.* Washington, D.C., October 3, 1968. P. S12041.

INDEX

Abstract thought, 71
Adams, E. Sherman, 147
Adams, Henry, 8–11
Agnew, Vice-Pres. Spiro, 49
Agrarian environment, diagrammed, 72
Agrarian institutions, obsolete, 26
Agrarian mind, 70–73
Agriculture, Dept. of, farm subsidies, 41–44, 92
budget, 43–44
Aid To Dependent Children, 148
Allen, Dr. James E., 47
Alliance For Progress, 22
American Institute of Aeronautics and Astronautics, 29
American Medical Association, 149–151, 155
Amherst College, 49–51
Anderson, O. W., 154
Arvida, 178–180

Bailey, Steven K., 47
Bangkok, 14
Barbados Development Board, 16
Bedford-Stuyvesant, 122
Benn, Anthony Wedgewood, 128

Berger, Peter, 39
Black Power, 67
Body buffer zone, 64–65
Bogle, John C., 171
Boring machines, 186
Brain drain, 14, 18–20, 78
Brotzman, Rep. Donald G., 131
Brown, Rep. Clarence J., 145
Budget, Bureau of, 92, 115
Budgets
and policies, 92–93
zero-base, 115–116
Bullet, The, quoted, 38
Bushel, Arthur, 148–149
Butler, Robert N., 155

Calhoun, John B., 63
Campbell, Rev. Ernest T., 39
Cantor, Arnold, 102–103
Chicago Tribune, quoted, 42
Child development
depends upon locality, 109–110
Chisholm, Rep. Shirley, 122–123
City
physical shell, 5
populations and densities, 4–5, 31–32
as an ecological system, Preface, 3, 76–77, 81, 156, 194
Greek and Roman, 67–68

Clark, Kenneth B., 32
Clifford, Clark M., 137–138
Coal miners, 111–112
Cohen, Wilbur J., 89, 142
Collins, George R., 45
Columbia, Maryland, 172
Columbia University, 44–46
Comprehensive insurance, 135–136, 150–151
Computor Input Corporation, 14
Conference 2020, 175–177
Consolidated Edison Co., 107–108
Contradictions, 54
Copper, ores, 20
Cornell University, 168
Cornwall-on-Hudson, 107–108
Coulanges, Fustel de, 67–68
Crowding, 60–67
Crozier, Michel, 55–56, 59
Cullum, Mollie Porter, 119
Cultural diversity, 59, 67
Culture, as survival mechanism, 64
Culture shock, 66

Davis, Arthur Vining, 178–180
Debt peonage, 21–23
Defense, Dept. of
  expenditures, 137, 140
  health care, 151
Deindividuation, 65
Dennis, Cannon Walter, 39
Douglas, Sen. Paul H., 88, 114
Draftees
  health of, 153–154

Eastland, Sen. James O., 42
Ecology, urban, Preface, 3, 12, 56–59, 71, 75–77, 154–155
Economic development, 20–24
Economic growth
  penalizes local government, 103–104, 184
  as national policy, 111–113
Econo-technic networks, 121, 125, 129
Education, expenditures for, 84
Edwards, Lawrence K., 187–188
Einstein, Albert, 6–7, 12, 155, 189
Eisenhower, Pres. Dwight D., 112–113, 115
Electricity, production, 9–10
Ellul, Jacques, 62
Employer of last resort, 133, 146
Energy, sources, 9–11
Engel, Joseph H., 29
Environment, function of, 71–72, 124, 175
  public, 109–110
Epps, Richard W., 105, 108

Farm, as social security, 73, 79
  ecological equation, 77
Farm subsidies, 40–44, 91–92, 99, 141, 153
  number, 43
  size, 43
  taxes paid, 99
  wages, 141
Federal Government, tax collections, 82–83, 87, 103, 105

Federal Reserve Bank, 112–113
Feudal system, 190–191
Finch, Robert, 90, 149–150
Flat Earth Society, 160
Flax, Alexander H., 113–114
Flowers, Roy, 42
Food stamps, 40–42
Fong, Sen. Hiram, 131
Foreign policy, is domestic policy, 25
Forman, James, 39
Fort Gordon, Georgia, 139
Freeman, Orville, 40, 74
Friedman, Milton, 142–144
Fulbright, Sen. William, Frontispiece, 48–49
Full Employment Act, 112
Fuller, R. Buckminster, Introduction, 6, 117, 168

Gallup Poll, 37, 106, 133
Gardner, John W., 146
Gemini III, 27
Geographic place, 125
Ghetto, a Federal responsibility, 105, 194–195
Glasgow, Robert W., 30
Glass, H. Bentley, 153
Globalization, 13, 58, 78, 121, 125, 184, 190, 195
Gordon, Kermit, 91–92
Gore, Sen. Albert, 127
Gottmann, Jean, 180
Great Southwest Corp., 119–120, 180
Greenhouse, The, 119, 180
Greer, Scott, 31
Griffin, Sen. Robert, 43–44

Grimm, Wayne, 138–139
Gross National Product, 33, 84, 139–140, 197
Guaranteed annual income, 134, 142–144, 147

Harlem, 105–106
Hartke, Sen. Vance, 152–153
Harvard University, 47–48
Haskins, Kenneth W., 125–126
Health
of draftees, 153–154
and poverty, 148–149, 154
Health, Education and Welfare, Dept. of
expenditures, 95–97
welfare programs, 97–98
Helicopters, 35–36, 114, 197
High-speed rail, 180, 187–188
Hill, Guy, 108–109
Hong Kong, 16–17
Horn, Francis H., 30–31
Horn, Steven, 127
Housing
construction methods, 166–171
disposable, 167–169
investment capital, 171–173
Howe, Marton W., 33
Hurricane barrier, 185
Hypocrisy, 61, 70

Income, per capita, 20–21, 195–196
Income tax, 71, 80
and talent, 100
collections, 101
and economic growth, 103–104

India, exports, 16
Institutions, 121
  networks, 128, 157–158, 166
Institutional status, 128, 166
Inter-Governmental Co-operation Act of 1968, 85
International development, 191–193
Investment capital, housing, 171–173
Irvine Principle, 164–165, 172, 177
Irvine Ranch Co., 162–164, 171

Japan, investments abroad, 19
Javas of Queen Island, 54
Javits, Sen. Jacob, 131
Johnson Administration, 35, 74, 96–97, 152, 182
Johnson, G. Lawton, 16
Johnson, Pres. Lyndon B., 37, 86, 88, 153, 169
Johnson, Ralph J., 169
Johnston, Rhode Island, 130

Kastenmeier, Rep. Robert W., 102–103
Kennedy, Sen. Edward, 127
Keyes, Kenneth, 38
Kidney machines, 152–153
Kinzel, August F., 64–65
Kleenex architecture, 171
K.O.B.-T.V., station, 131
Knowles, John H., 150–151
Kuykendall, Rep. Dan, 48

La dolce vita, 191
Land
  as commodity, 161
  as public utility, 164–165, 172, 182
  consumption, 181–182
  leasing, 162–165
  management, 161, 162
  management companies, 164, 166, 171–173
  rotation of use, 164, 173
  shaping, 186–187
  urbanized, 181
Land ownership, 128
Laredo, 15
Lindsay, Mayor John, 88–89, 106
Litton Industries, 17
Liuzzo, Viola, 28
Local government, and farmer, 71–73, 80
  number, 82
  taxes collected, 83, 99–101
  responsibility, 82, 104
Long, Sen. Russell B., 127
Lorenz, Konrad, 63–64
Love, through exposure, 66
Lowndes County, 28

Madden, Rep. Ray J., 41
Malthusian-Darwinian-Marxian Thesis, 116–117
Marx, Karl, 116–117
Mayo, Robert, 115
McNamara, Robert S., 20–21, 195
Medicaid, 150
Medical care, 138
Medicenters of America, 155–156
Megalopolis, 180
Mental illness, 62–65, 69

Middle class, incomes and public responsibilities, 104–107
Military
suppression by, 21–22, 189
policy, 113–114
spending, 113–117
health care, 138–151
Military-Industrial-Complex, 115, 137–138
Miller, Herman, 69, 100
Morningside Park, 44–46
Muskie, Sen. Edmund S., 24

Narragansett Bay, 185
National Association of Home Builders, 168–169
National Commission on Urban Problems, 88
National Kidney Foundation, 153
National sovereignty, 125, 129, 190–191
Neanderthal man, 159
Negative income tax, 142–144, 147
Negro population, 31–32, 89
vote, 90
Neighborhood Youth Corps, 130
Neiman-Marcus, 119
New towns, 166–171
industrial sponsors, 166, 172–173
New York City, budget, 107
New York Times, The, 50
Niebuhr, Reinhold, 39–40
Nixon Administration, 74, 85–86, 88, 152

Nixon, Pres. Richard, 50, 97, 127, 145, 146, 151

O'Brien, Ralph, 17
Ocean Hill-Brownsville, 105–106
O'Leary, Jeremiah, 2
Organization-man, 70
Overmyer, D., Co., 169

Participatory democracy, 123–124
Patronage, 130–131
Peabody Coal Co., 186
Pearson, Drew, 127
Pell, Sen. Claiborne, 180
Penn Central Railroad, 180
Pentagon
hot line, 36
contracts, 48–49
spending, 82, 100, 113–117, 195
policy, 113–114
Piel, Gerard, quoted, 9
Plimpton, Calvin H., 50–51
Police, suppression by, 21
Population
of cities, 4–5, 31–32
urban-rural, 70
classified by income, 140–141
Poor
number, 132
classified, 132–133
eligible for assistance, 146
Porter, Sylvia, 139
Poverty
and health, 154
cause of death, 148–149
circle of, 147–148

Poverty (*cont.*)
classified, 132
incomes, 140–142
programs, 130–140, 146–147
roots of, 90, 140
war on, 131
Prebisch, Raul, 192
President's National Advisory Commission on Civil Disorders, 31–33, 35, 50, 131
Priorities, 142
established by budgets, 92–93, 103
Property
as basis of security, 68–73, 175, 191
tax, 99–102, 105, 165, 184
Providence Evening Bulletin, 130
Proxmire, Sen. William, 114–116
Psychological programming, 58
Public utility, land, 164, 172, 182
Pucinski, Cong. Roman C., 91
Pushkrev, Boris S., 176

Rand Corporation, 29–30
Raskin, A. H., 107
Reagan, Gov. Ronald, 49, 127
Rebellion, 20–24
Religion, 33–37
as industry, 39–40
Republican Campaign Committee, 151
Rennie, Thomas A. C., 62
Representative government, 121–124, 126–128

Research and development, 78
budget, 113–114
policy, 114
Reserve Officer Training Corps, 47
Resource, international systems, 13–19, 125
Resources, natural, 18, 121
derived by technology, 18, 129
agrarian, 21–23
Revolt, in underdeveloped countries, 20–21
Rhodes, Rep. John J., 131
Richter, Kurt, 63
Riot control
as big business, 34–35
seminars, 36
Rockefeller, John D. III, 51
Rockefeller, Gov. Nelson, 90–91, 175–176, 196
Rolph, Earl R., 148
Roper, Elmo, 176
Roth, Rep. William V., 147
Rowe, 108
Russell, Major Robert A., 33, 37
Ryan, Cong. William F., 35

Saunders, J. A. H., 16–17
Scarcity, 189
as reality, 71, 142
Scarsdale, 105–106
Schlesinger, Arthur M., Sr., 8, 12
Scott, Douglas, 30
Security, basis of, 68–69, 166, 175, 191
Self-sufficiency, 70–73

Servan-Schrieber, Jean Jacques, 19–20
Shaw, Dr. Robert H., 38
Shenton, Samuel, 160
Simeons, A. T. W., 60
Social awareness, 137–139
Social constraints, 60–61
Social inequities, and geographic boundaries, 109–110
Social institutions, as survival mechanisms, 4
Social Security, 79, 93–97, 135–136
 budgets, 94–97
 premiums, 83
Social status, 125
Society of responsibility, 12–13
 function of, 72
South Kingstown, 109
Standard Oil Co., 126–127
Steingut, Stanley, 148
Sterling, Morton A., 170
Stikker, Dirk U., 191–192
Stone walls, 175
Subsidies, 141–148, 153
Suburban development, 176
Sunnyhill Mine, 111
Sunset International Petroleum Co., 170
SWAT, 32–33
Swick, Charles J., 100
Symington, Sen. Stuart, 114
Systems analysis, 29

Talent
 as basis of security, 69, 71
 and taxation, 100
Tax base, of local governments, 99–110

Taxation, of farms, 72–73, 80
Technological revolution, and social revolution, 23
Technology
 and social context, 11
 defined by Ellul, 62
Territory, 165–166
 represented, 123
 and security, 125, 191
Thompson, Wilbur, 103, 184
Tiernan, Rep. Robert O., 138
Time zoning, 177–178
Tower, Sen. John, 151
Toynbee, Arnold, 11–12, 189
Transitron Electronics Corporation, 15
Tristan da Cunha, 1–2
Truman, Pres. Harry S, 149
Trust funds, 93–97, 136
Tucson, 14–15
Tunnel digging, 186
Turner, Frederick, 8
Twin plant, concept, 14–15
Tydings, Sen. Joseph, 106
Tyson, Cyril D., 134

Underdeveloped countries
 manpower, 13–19
 wages, 13–19
 élites, 190–191
Unemployed, hard core, 138–139, 157
Unified Budget, 95–97
United Fund, 143
Unruh, Jesse, 127
Upgrading, 24–26
Urban Coalition, 133–134

Urban Ecology
diagrammed, 75–76
anti-entropic, 76
equation, 76–77
Urban mind, needed, 74–77
Urbanization, defined, Preface
as social process, 12–13, 120–121
technological potential, 25
as ecological process, 56–59
U.S. Army Corps of Engineers, 185
U.S. Conference of Mayors, 89
U.S. Post Office Dept., 130–131
User charges, 100

Van Arsdale, Harry, 107
Vietnam, 22–23, 32, 36, 46, 184
Vietnam War, 184
costs, 153, 158–159, 195
VISTA slogan, 50

Wagner, Susan, 38
Wall Street Journal, The, 134
War, is obsolete, Preface, 13
Washington Post, The, 134

Watson, Philip E., 100
Weinberger, Caspar, 102
Welfare
expenditures, 83, 91, 98, 135, 144–145
residency requirements, 91
payments to farmers, 91–92
for middle class, 135
overhead, 143
Whitehead, A. N., 111
Williams, John H., 108
Williams, Sen. John W., 41–42
Wilson, Rep. Bob, 151
Wolff, Rep. Lester L., 126
World, one, 121
Wynne, Mrs. Angus Jr., 119–120

Young, Rev. Andrew, 28

Zajonc, Robert B., 66
Zero-base budgeting, 115–116
Zimbardo, Philip G., 65
Zoning, 167
time, 177–178

About The Author

Presently Chairman of the Department of Geography of the University of Rhode Island, Dr. Higbee has had a distinguished academic career and an equally distinguished one "in the field." As Senior Agronomist for the U.S. Department of Agriculture, he was from 1938 to 1947 Consultant in Agronomy to the governments of Brazil, Guatemala, Peru, Ecuador, Nicaragua, and El Salvador. *A Question of Priorities* is the result of five years of research, supported in part by a grant from the Twentieth Century Fund, which he has served as Research Director for its studies on the agricultural revolution and America's public environment. He is a consultant on land utilization to the Brookings Institution, a member of the Technical Advisory Committee of the New England Council, and a member of the Technical Advisory Committee to the U.S. Congressional Committee on the Quality of the Environment. He has participated in urban policy conferences sponsored by the Brookings Institution and in working seminars with professional city managers at conferences sponsored jointly by the Brookings Institution and the International City Managers Association in some twenty American cities. He lives with his wife and young daughter in Kingston, Rhode Island.

301.3 Higbee, Edward.
H

A question of priorities

c.l.

DATE	ISSUED TO

c.1
301.3 Higbee, Edward.
H   A question of priorities.